ENDORSI

Jesse and Amy Shamp are one of those power couples in the body of Christ I just love to be around. They bring God's miracle-working power wherever they go, and I'm so excited that they decided to teach what they know to the rest of us. Read. Grow. Be inspired and empowered!

DR. ROBERTS LIARDON
Roberts Liardon Ministries
Embassy International Church

What is the Holy Spirit saying in this hour? He is speaking loudly to us about coming up into the next level accessing and living in the realm of God's glory where all things are possible! Are there any next-generation prophetic voices that I recommend you listen to and partake of their ministry? The answer is, "YES!" Two of these emerging voices with a proven track record are my friends Jesse and Amy Shamp. I have had the honor of knowing Jesse's family and speaking confirmation and blessings over this anointed man of God. It is my joy and honor to commend to you their book, *Miracles in the Glory,* filled with exhilarating testimonies and practical steps on how you can practice His presence and be a miracle worker yourself.

JAMES W. GOLL
Founder of God Encounters Ministries and
GOLL Ideation LLC
International Speaker, Author, Singer,
and Communications Trainer

Jesse and Amy Shamp desire to see each believer living a life filled with miracles, empowered by the anointing of the Holy Spirit. In this book you will read many powerful testimonies that will encourage you to embrace the newness of God in all of His glory. I challenge you to not only read this book, but receive an impartation from it, and witness *Miracles in the Glory* in your own personal life!

JOSHUA MILLS
Author, *Moving in Glory Realms*
International Glory Ministries
Palm Springs, California
www.JoshuaMills.com

Miracles in the Glory by Amy and Jesse Shamp is a powerful, faith-building book that is full of revelatory insights, biblical truth, and personal testimony. Your passion for God and His Kingdom will get stirred for sure as you read through its pages.

DR. PATRICIA KING
Founder, Patricia King Ministries

Miracles in the Glory by Jesse and Amy Shamp is one of the most faith-building books I've read. Your faith to believe God for miracles and healing power will most certainly be taken to a new level when reading this book. The testimonies from Jesse and Amy's lives and the lives of others are sure to catapult you into a new dimension of glory. I am so excited and can't wait to hear the testimonies of healings, signs, and wonders from those who read this book and get activated into the miraculous! There is such a fresh wind of glory on this book! I just couldn't put it down! God is certainly on the move in their lives and yours!

DR. KAYE BEYER
We Care For You Ministries
Tampa, Florida
www.wcfym.com

There's a certain kind of book I look for when I really want to dig in and learn things from the Lord. First, it's got to be easy reading and not too complex. Then it has to be filled throughout with scriptural support for what is being taught. And finally, it needs lots and LOTS of personal stories by the authors, so the reader can be immersed in what is being said. The reader must feel he was there! That's where real learning and understanding happen. Well, you guessed it, *Miracles in the Glory* by Jesse and Amy Shamp is exactly that kind of book. You're going to love it. Get your copy, and buy one for a friend while you're at it.

STEVE SHULTZ
Founder, THE ELIJAH LIST
www.elijahlist.com

Miracles in the Glory is an inspirational read. I love hearing testimonies of believers stepping out in their calling from a dream encounter. I was blessed by Jesse sharing his testimony of obeying the call out from his own dream encounter. I believe it is essential for every believer to walk in the revelatory understanding of Colossians 1:27: *"To them God willed to make known what are the riches of the glory of this mystery among the Gentiles: which is Christ in you, the hope of glory."* You will be intrigued with the writings of the different stories of how God raised up the generals as an example of what the body of Christ is going to look like corporately in these coming days. Amy explains the different dimensions of glory and gives examples of miracles that occur as a result of their ministry. I believe every believer in Christ should have a copy of this book. Congratulations, Jesse and Amy. You are such blessings to the body of Christ.

ADAM F. THOMPSON
Prophetic minister and international author
www.voiceoffireministries.org

Jesse and Amy Shamp have craftfully carved out, with the pens of ready writers, a phenomenal book full of substance. This book can easily prepare a scaffolding for you to build your own faith upon in order to walk in the miracle power of the Holy Spirit for the rest of your lives. Rich in church history, revelatory teaching of Scriptures, and their own powerful testimonies, you will receive an impartation for making Jesus famous in your lifetime if you apply the principles they teach. I highly recommend this read to you, as well as suggest it as a great tool for churches to study corporately in Bible study groups!

MUNDAY MARTIN
Contagious Love International
www.contagiousloveintl.com

MIRACLES
in the
GLORY

MIRACLES
in the
GLORY

UNLOCKING THE REALM OF
SIGNS AND WONDERS THROUGH
THE PRESENCE OF GOD

JESSE & AMY SHAMP

DESTINY IMAGE® PUBLISHERS, INC.
P.O. Box 310, Shippensburg, PA 17257-0310
"Promoting Inspired Lives."

This book and all other Destiny Image and Destiny Image Fiction books are available at Christian bookstores and distributors worldwide.

For more information on foreign distributors, call 717-532-3040.
Or reach us on the Internet: www.destinyimage.com

ISBN 13 TP: 978-0-7684-4290-8
ISBN 13 EBook: 978-0-7684-4291-5
ISBN LP - 978-0-7684-4292-2
ISBN HC- 978-0-7684-4293-9

For Worldwide Distribution, Printed in the U.S.A.
1 2 3 4 5 6 / 21 20 19 18

CONTENTS

FOREWORD

When I am interested in reading a new book, I have to ask myself several questions: Is the life of the author consistent with the message of the book I am reading? Is this person's ministry supportive of the declarations of the book I hold in my hands? If I cannot say yes to both of these questions, regardless of the content, I will pass on reading it.

In the case of *Miracles in the Glory* by Jesse and Amy Shamp, I can personally attest a positive yes to both of these questions. I have witnessed the lives of both Jesse and Amy for years and not only are they both anointed and appointed ministers in our day and age, but they are associates and graduates of the Kingdom Life Institute with Global Fire Ministries International. Both Jesse and Amy are pure vessels of revelation and power and are forerunners in this generation of a rising, new-breed army of God that brings fresh power and glory through the ministry of signs, wonders, and miracles.

I've watched Jesse grow from a young student with Kingdom Life Institute to a progressive and hungry young minister who not only has a solid biblical grid for understanding the "mechanics" of the glory, but is someone who demonstrates it on a regular basis.

The book you hold in your hands is not only a testimony to the supernatural, but a guide to activating it in your personal life and the lives of others. There are many who can preach and teach but lack demonstration of the miraculous. The apostle Paul said:

> *With the power of signs and wonders, [and all of it] in the power of the Spirit. So starting from Jerusalem and as far away as Illyricum, I have fully preached the Gospel [faithfully preaching the good news] of Christ where it had not before been preached* (Romans 15:19 AMP).

Full Gospel preaching is preaching the gospel with the demonstration of signs, wonders, and miracles in the Holy Spirit and both Jesse and Amy do this.

I love this book because it declares without reservation that the Kingdom of God is here in power; we are part of it as normal believers.

I love this book because it challenges us to reach higher for the deep things of God, and that it not only leaves us there, but gives us a handle on how to apprehend it.

I love this book because it is a call to all for a spiritual reevaluation of how we have been doing things as the church. It's time to believe for more!

I love this book because practical faith is clearly presented as being anchored in the unseen realm while living in the natural realm. Once we open this door by faith, with understanding, we are standing on the launching pad for a rocket ride into the glory realm!

I love this book because it leaves me hungry for more and not to settle for what I have as an international minister myself. I am always pushing myself into the deep—and this book inspires me to go deeper.

I can assure you that as you read this book, your life will change and this is why I can fully recommend it to you without reservation.

Read it slowly and digest its content. The results, I believe, will be nothing less than *Miracles in the Glory* for you!

DR. JEFF JANSEN
Global Fire Ministries International
Senior Pastor, Global Fire Church
Author of *Glory Rising, Furious Sound of Glory, Enthroned*

CHAPTER 1

THE POWER OF THE SECRET PLACE

by Jesse

*When you pray, go into your room, and when
you have shut your door, pray to your Father
who is in the secret place; and your Father
who sees in secret will reward you openly.*
—MATTHEW 6:6

What the Bible refers to as the "secret place" is where you get alone with God and spend time in fellowship with Him. The secret place is any private place; it could be an office, your house, your bedroom, or your closet. It is wherever you are alone with God. It is the place where you experience God's manifest presence, where you encounter all that He is in order that you may reveal His glory and power to others. In the overflow of His presence, favor and supernatural power come as a result. The depth of your hunger will lead to the greatest depths of His presence in your life.

Like so many pioneers we talk about in the church world today—revivalists from the past, history makers, and those who truly accomplished something incredible for God and for their generation—it all began for them in the secret place.

That's where it began for me, where everything in my life changed. There was an acceleration, a supernatural power, and a divine favor that launched me into my destiny. Before I ever met my beautiful wife Amy, I always knew that there was a call of God on my life even from a young age. I used to lay on my bed at night, being only ten years of age, envisioning myself preaching before crowds of people—and I would continually tell the Lord, "Please use someone else. I can't do it. How do You expect me to preach in front of all these people?"

Throughout the years, I knew in my heart that there was a call of God on my life, and in some ways, it was like a heavy burden that I couldn't get away from. One night the Lord gave me a dream. In this dream, I was holding a microphone, preaching in a church and people were receiving miracles as I prayed for them. I knew that the Lord had set me apart for His use. Yet I felt so afraid to say yes to the call!

I grew up in a Christian home. My parents loved the Lord and they were what some would call "radical God-chasers." They would go into dangerous neighborhoods to share the gospel of Jesus and win souls. They were on fire for the Lord and were looking for something real in God, something more than dead, lifeless religion. They wanted the real thing, no matter how great the persecution attached to it.

NEVER THE SAME

I remember the day when my father and another pastor came together at our home talking about a man named David Hogan who was being used mightily by God, and who had raised the dead in Mexico. They began to pray and wrote a letter to David Hogan inviting him to come to our town to preach. David accepted the invitation. It was these three days of meetings that changed my family forever. We had never been exposed to anything supernatural, beyond speaking in tongues.

In these meetings when David ministered, there were notable miracles that took place. For example, there was a man who received a miracle from being crippled; he had been confined in a wheelchair for several years. There were so many people who received miracles, healing, and deliverance.

I will never forget the night David Hogan gave an altar call, inviting people to receive prayer for the baptism of the Holy Spirit. As I approached the altar for prayer, David instructed his younger son to pray for me. His son looked to be about twelve years of age, about as old as I was at the time. He reached out to me with a handkerchief in his hand and touched my chest, and the power of God went through my body like powerful electricity. Throughout the years of my life, I never forgot this experience! It was the first time that I was touched by the Holy Spirit!

My family was never the same. I remember my father received a visitation from the Lord that year and received a supernatural gold tooth. Many of his church friends and his dentist could hardly understand why God would do such a thing. My father's dentist kept asking him who was it that performed the dental work on his tooth, as he shook his head in disbelief. From then on, when my parents would minister to people, they would see people set free from demons and healed of illnesses such as cancer.

JESUS FULL OF LIGHT, GLORY, AND POWER

My parents would often bring missionaries into our home to stay. They usually ended up sleeping in my bedroom. Which I was never excited about. One night a man came to stay at our home. I had to sleep in my brother Charlie's room. I had a profound encounter with the Lord that night. I had fallen asleep and slipped into an encounter. My spirit was lifted into Heaven. Then I saw what looked like a man walking toward me—He was full of light, glory, and power. I knew it was Jesus! The closer He came to me the brighter and more powerful the glory became! I knew that the Lord was calling me, but at the time I refused to say yes.

When I was sixteen, I remember being so backslidden that I found myself exhausted with church. I told myself that I would never be a minister. I would say that I was definitely my youth pastor's worst nightmare during this season of my life. Yet, I'll never forget the day that a woman came to our church and told my mother that she wanted to pay for my father and I to go to India together. I argued to have my brother Charlie go in my place, complaining that I wasn't a preacher. But she insisted, telling me to go and observe. In her words, she said this trip had to do with my destiny and ministry in the future. She said that she had seen in a vision my father and I and another man going to India.

Much of what she saw in her vision came to pass, with great detail! One of the words of prophecy she gave was that during this trip, we would meet a boy named Dennis, with glasses. The word came to pass during the trip! Looking back, I can see that she had what we would call a *seer gift,* as she prophesied with great accuracy. There was a man who accompanied us on the trip named Gordon Jensen. You may even have heard one of his famous songs, entitled, "Written in Red." Gordon had played music for Benny Hinn for many years. One night while singing on the platform during one of Benny's crusades, Benny Hinn prophesied over him and the power of God fell on him. He then began to move in the healing anointing, coupled with an accurate *word of knowledge* gift, or a prophetic gift where the Lord would reveal to him details about a person's life.

As we were in India, I saw Gordon minister words of knowledge with great detail. Nearly every night, he would go into his hotel room to pray, and come out the next day with a list of names and conditions that he would call out in the crusades. The names were a bit difficult for Gordon to pronounce, as you can imagine them being Indian names that Americans are not quite accustomed to pronouncing. People would respond by name and come and be healed of tumors and blood diseases. One man testified that the doctors had given up on him after three attempts to surgically remove cancer. At the crusade, Gordon ministered to him and he later testified that the doctors could not find a trace of cancer.

Hindus and Muslims came to give their lives to the Lord. Many people were set free from demons and oppression, and countless salvations took place as my father and Gordon ministered side by side!

The trip had great impact on me throughout the years. Yet in my heart I was still wrestling with God. As much as I tried, I could not get away from the call to minister the gospel. I continually ran from the Lord, rebelling, doing all that I could to shake the feeling of being called by God; yet, God would not let me go.

I later began using drugs and alcohol, which led me to getting in trouble with the law. I was much like Jonah in the Bible, who fled from the call of God. The call was there, but it wasn't until my early twenties that I said "yes" to it. The Bible says that many are called, but few are chosen (see Matt. 22:14). I've always believed this Scripture to mean that few have said "yes" to obeying the call of God.

I had spent so many years running from the Lord, running from my call, from my divine purpose. It seemed that the more I ran, the more trouble I would find myself in. The enemy wanted to take my life so that he could stop me from entering into my divine destiny. I remember the day that I was, once again, placed in handcuffs and taken to jail. Suddenly it dawned on me that if I didn't surrender completely to the Lord, I would eventually be taken to prison or lose my life.

I had finally come to the place in my heart where I wanted more than what the world had to offer. I was given the opportunity to go through a drug rehabilitation program called Teen Challenge. The experience changed my life forever. I found a peace that had been missing in my life for so many years. I knew that a change had taken place inside me. I knew in my heart, that I had been set free from my past. As I would study God's Word and pray, I could feel the power of the Holy Spirit come upon me like waves.

I can honestly say that it was the best time of my life, but also the worst time of my life. I had hit rock bottom. I was in a place of brokenness, in a place where I didn't know if God could do anything with the mess that I had made of my life. Yet, I discovered that the Lord was with me in my brokenness. Every day, I began to draw closer and closer to the Holy Spirit. God's presence became everything to me and helped me get through what I was facing in that season of my life. After completing Teen Challenge, I was eager to spend time with the Lord in the secret place. I wanted to press in for an encounter with the Lord like I had never previously experienced.

THE SECRET PLACE

Before my wife, Amy, and I met, God was preparing me in the secret place, and God was preparing her as well! I believe many overlook the importance of the secret place and the vital role that it plays into our own individual destinies. The secret place is where we go from being just called to chosen. It's the place where our destinies are birthed, where we empty ourselves of all that we are and allow the Lord to fill us and prepare us for His use!

I had made up my mind that I was going to press in and encounter the Lord. I had such a hunger that was rising in me to know the Lord. I was so desperate. There are many Christians who have desired to know the Lord in a powerful way, yet they have never allowed themselves to become desperate for a deep touch from Him. There is something about hunger that draws Heaven to you. I was at that place of spiritual hunger to know Him, to know the Holy Spirit in the way that others said they knew Him! I desired to know the Holy Spirit the way I heard others talk about Him.

I decided to go on a twenty-day fast. During that time, I began praying in the Spirit for hours every day! I would push myself to pray a little bit more each day. As I would ask God for the fire to come, the fire of the Holy Spirit would start to fall on me. Each day, the fire would be even stronger. would meditate on Scriptures, such as Acts 2:2 where it says that the Holy Spirit entered the upper room like a mighty rushing wind. It was my desire to encounter the Holy Spirit the way the apostles did in the upper room! I wanted that very same fire! Each day, I would pray as long as I could, which took a lot of discipline at first. Then I began to notice that I was praying with ease. Instead of prayer seeming like a chore, I couldn't wait until I could get away from everyone and everything and spend time with the Lord.

As the days went by, the Holy Spirit's presence became so real and tangible. There were even times when I felt electricity flowing into my body as the Holy Spirit was brooding over me. As the presence of the Holy Spirit would come upon me, all I could do was bask in His presence as He would fill me over and over again! The Holy Spirit began to wash over me so strongly that all I could do was weep in His presence uncontrollably. This would happen to me for several hours a day, where

I would be in the presence of the Holy Spirit, and all I could do was weep and ask God to send me to the nations. I knew this to be a burden for souls that the Lord was placing on my life. The Bible says, *"Ask of Me and I will give You the nations for Your inheritance..."* (Ps. 2:8).

Suddenly there was a passion burning within me to minister the gospel in the nations. It became the very cry of my heart—and continues to be. There was a fire in my heart and in my spirit that I had never known before. Day after day, the Holy Spirit was visiting me. It felt like it was just the beginning of what was available to me in God. I knew there was so much more that the Lord wanted me to experience, so much more He wanted to reveal to me. There was such a mystery in the sense that every day seemed so fresh and new. I purposed in my heart that I was not going to be satisfied with a season of knowing the Lord, nor be satisfied with merely an encounter. I felt as if I had barely tasted of what was available. I knew that if I continued to press in and continued to be hungry, that God was going to reveal Himself to me according to my hunger and sheer desire to know Him.

A DIVINE SEASON

It was such a divine season in my life that it is difficult to express through words. I began to truly know and bond with the Holy Spirit. He became so real to me, not just as a feeling or an atmosphere, but as real as a person or companion. I understand why Kathryn Kuhlman often referred to the Holy Spirit as her best friend. She relied upon the Holy Spirit to move upon the people in her meetings, to perform healings and miracles!

I've tried desperately to make this season of my life of the secret place into a lifestyle. I've returned continually to this place of being filled and refilled by the Holy Spirit. We must make it a priority to return to that place of spiritual hunger, forever returning to that foundation of discovering Him over and over again. Daily I remind myself that it's all about knowing and experiencing Him!

I was only twenty years of age when I had decided to say yes to the call of God on my life. It was the greatest decision that I could have made. Being in this season, I was encountering the Lord in ways that I never thought possible. It was amazing, yet I felt that there was still something missing or out of place. Though I had always felt that there was a call of God on my life, I had never received a commissioning word from a prophet to confirm my call. I began to doubt if I was truly called. I thought to myself that if I was truly called, God would confirm it through a true prophet. I prayed, "Lord, if You have called me into the ministry, then You will have Jeff Jansen prophesy over me everything that I am called to do at his church in Murfreesboro, Tennessee." I told the Lord it had to be that Tuesday night or I wouldn't go into the ministry.

You may think, *Who do you think you are, talking to the Lord like that?* But I was serious when I said yes to the call of God, and I was believing for a word from God to confirm it! I had been to Jeff's church on so many Tuesday nights. I had been to nearly every Tuesday service since Jeff started his church—but this night, I was believing for God to answer the cry of my heart and to answer my prayer.

The service began and suddenly Jeff called me out in front of the church and prophesied over me the call of God on my life; he spoke out everything that I was called to do. The word was about the calling of the nations, about a mantle for miracles, signs, and wonders. Much of what my wife and I are doing now came as a result of that prophetic word. Even this book that you are reading now came from the prophetic word spoken over my life and destiny that night! It was a divine commissioning, a kairos moment, a mantle for the miraculous that was released on my life for a divine purpose!

Looking back, I can see that the Lord was depositing so much in me in that particular season for my destiny. There was such favor and power that came on my life, and I know that the Lord will do this for you as He has for me, as you journey into the secret place with God!

CHAPTER 2

THE HEALING ANOINTING

by Jesse

The Bible says that God *"is a rewarder of those who diligently seek Him"* (Heb. 11:6). There is something about pursuing the Lord with all that we have, not only in prayer, or in worship, but in the study of His Word. God begins to reward us as we pursue Him through His Word!

> *It is the glory of God to conceal a thing: but the honour of kings is to search out a matter* (Proverbs 25:2 KJV).

Revelation comes through seeking and searching out. When the Spirit of revelation comes, it awakens us in areas of our lives that we didn't know we were asleep! As we study the gifts and the importance of the healing anointing, I believe something will be deposited and awakened within you!

*For to one is given by the Spirit the word of wisdom;
to another the word of knowledge by the same Spirit;
to another faith by the same Spirit; to another gifts of
healing by the same Spirit* (1 Corinthians 12:8-9 KJV).

Paul the apostle begins to list the gifts of the Spirit in First
Corinthians chapter 12. Paul mentions the gifts of healing, but he also
mentions *"gifts of healings"* as well (1 Cor. 12:28). The words "gifts" and
"healings" are plural.

It may be that there are gifts of healings because there are different kinds of diseases. For example, I have noticed in my own ministry,
as well as in the ministry of others who have these gifts of healings in
operation in their lives and ministries, that when it comes to healings,
in some areas I have more success than in other areas. Other ministers
have concurred that this is also true in their ministries.[1]

Throughout revival history we can see that many called to the healing ministry had a "signature healing," where God used them greatly in
one area of healing more than others.

SIGNATURE HEALINGS

One of the signature healings that William Branham saw regularly was
the healing of crossed eyes. I believe this was, in many ways, connected
to the loss of his daughter. Branham's daughter, Sharon Rose, was diagnosed with what the doctor called "tubercular meningitis." Because of
the pain of the disease, her eyes become crossed. She later died from
the disease.[2]

The devastation of losing his daughter caused a greater compassion for those dealing with this particular ailment. Nearly everyone
Branham encountered with this type of disease, he carried and released
compassion for those suffering. He had an incredible success rate.

Smith Wigglesworth was especially blessed with a ministry to people who suffered from seizures of various kinds. When people with epilepsy were brought to his meetings, Wigglesworth knew there would be a revival because they were nearly always healed.[3]

Stephen Jeffreys had an incredible anointing when it came to seeing healing with those suffering from rheumatoid arthritis. He had an anointing for creative miracles! Lester Sumrall wrote about the great evangelist and the raw power that he operated in.

In the middle of the service, Stephen (Jeffreys) would jump off the platform, run to the back, curse rheumatoid arthritis, for example, and scream, "Come out of him." People said you could hear the bones pop for approximately thirty feet around as the person's bones began to relocate.[4]

I believe in many healing ministries; there are those who find themselves more fruitful in some areas of healing than others. It may be that we are more compassionate with those suffering from certain illnesses, as Branham was. It could also be that the ministers they are or were associated with, caused them to operate in a similar mantle, as it occurred with Elijah and Elisha. Elisha saw similar manifestations that the prophet Elijah saw in his ministry. Certain giftings and manifestations will always follow a ministry, and some have the ability, as Elijah did, to raise up others in the same mantle or anointing! All it takes is one impartation, and a person's ministry is never the same.

One of the greatest soul-winners, T.L. Osborn, knew that if he saw healing and miracles, then he would see souls come into the Kingdom. He testified about how he went to India and couldn't see any healings or any breakthrough with souls being saved. That was until Osborn encountered a man name William Branham who was preaching in Portland, Oregon. He saw many come to Christ that night, and many healings took place in the meeting. As T.L. Osborn sat in the meeting, he said that he heard ten thousand voices over his head, saying, "You can do that!" T.L. Osborn received an impartation that night in the meeting and went on to have one of the greatest soul-winning ministries of his generation![5]

I have always believed in the power of impartation. It is something spiritual that has been handed down from generation to generation; it's something we can trace back to the early church fathers! My wife and I received an impartation from Todd Bentley for seeing deafness healed. This is a signature healing that Todd has had throughout his ministry. Suddenly, my wife and I noticed a significant increase in seeing deaf ears open. In fact, we saw healings and even creative miracles for ears, in every meeting we did for months!

We should place value in impartation! Yet, it's important that we find our own voice in the process and our own identity in what God has called us to. Every gift may operate differently according to the calling and anointing that God places on that individual. Every individual has his or her own sound or voice of expression!

Those who are called to the healing anointing may have an area where God is using them greatly, and we may find that we have an anointing for that particular disease or illness. Yet, we should always be willing to allow ourselves to grow in that anointing.

I love something that Bill Johnson said in an interview with Randy Clark as they were talking about the breakthroughs they had seen in the healing anointing. Bill Johnson said, "To me, the sad part is to think that someone who has an anointing for one thing just stays there instead of using that as an experiment to springboard into something else. ...If you're getting breakthrough with leg lengthening, then why not look for other injuries to the leg, for example, bones that didn't heal in the leg, and go for that?"[6]

We should always be willing to press into those breakthroughs in healing, that way we are always learning and growing!

I want to bring you on a journey with me to show you how I stepped into the healing anointing. I feel that the more we study the gifts and receive light and revelation on the subject of gifts, the more is unlocked within us! It causes a stirring inside us and a holy desire. I've found that each time I return to the foundation of the gifts there is more awakened in me! There is something about desiring to see more of the gifts in our lives and developing a hunger for them. The Bible says to *"earnestly desire and cultivate the spiritual gifts"* (1 Cor. 14:1 AMP). I've always felt that it is the highest honor when God uses us as vessels of power so that God can reach through us and heal others!

Though I had some exposure to the healing anointing, I found that I knew very little about where to begin to minister healing to others. I knew that it was possible because I had seen others operate in that kind of power. Yet, my first initial thought was, where do I begin? In my heart, I wanted nothing more than to see people healed, delivered, and set free by the power of God's anointing. Being so eager to see the miraculous, I read every book I could find that had to do with miracles and the healing anointing. I read book after book by all the great generals and pioneers, such as Aimee Semple McPherson, John G. Lake, R.W. Schambach, Smith Wigglesworth, and many others. I studied all the great men and women of God whom God used so powerfully in the healing ministry. I saw that they all began by acting on simple faith, so I decided that if I prayed for the sick with unwavering faith, I would get the same results!

> *And these signs will follow those who believe...they will lay hands on the sick, and they will recover* (Mark 16:17-18).

Every believer is called to see healings and miracles. It's hardwired in our very DNA as sons and daughters of the Most High God to move in the miraculous. That is not to say that every believer is called to have a healing ministry or be upon a platform. Yet, the Word of God promises us, that if we believe, we will cast out devils and heal the sick! It's important that we recognize that the Great Commission is both a promise and a command! Seeing the sick healed is what every believer is called to, not just five-fold ministry gifts, not just the man or woman of God upon great platforms, but every believer is to play a part in the Great Commission. This is what Jesus commanded the body of Christ collectively to accomplish!

When we begin to cultivate evangelism in our churches as well as in our daily lives, we will see regions transformed, and the nations will become our inheritance (see Ps. 2:8). It's God's desire to mobilize the body of Christ to go out to the highways and byways and minister to the broken, to those afflicted with sickness, to those bound in drugs, and set them free! It was never God's intention to just raise up a few who would move in healing and deliverance; God's intention has always been to raise up an army that will expand His Kingdom on the earth! This is how we will begin to see whole cities transformed by the power of God! Now more than ever, it's time we become intentional about winning the lost!

I first began to learn how to minister healing and miracles not by ministering in churches, but through simple street evangelism. At first, I wasn't aware that I had an anointing for healing! It was raw faith that brought me to the beginning of my journey into the healing anointing. I decided that if I was hungry enough for the miraculous, then God would use me as He used others to heal the sick. I wanted so desperately to see people touched by the power of God in a way that was undeniable, in such a way that it would have to be God!

I took a few friends of mine and asked them if they wanted to hit the streets with me and pray for people for healing and miracles. So we did! We went to every mall, street, and grocery store that we could think of. We would spend hours praying for people. At first, I prayed for many people, yet didn't see any results. I could have easily been discouraged. Yet I kept believing for a breakthrough! There was a burning in my heart to see God perform healings and miracles. I encouraged myself not to give up. I remember thinking if I could just press in and pray for people until I saw one healing or one miracle, then God would continue to use me to see more!

One day, I saw a woman in the middle of a grocery aisle. The Lord gave me a word of knowledge for her back. He told me that for many years she had experienced pain in a disc in her lower back. I then shared the word of knowledge with her and asked her if I could pray for her. She agreed to allow me to pray for her. I could see that she was leaning on her shopping cart and using it to walk. As I prayed for her, I could feel a heat go through my hands. Suddenly, two loud *pops* came from her back and she stood up straight without any pain.

She then asked me if I had "psychic powers," and I told her that it was merely the power of Jesus flowing through me. Two of her friends had witnessed the healing that had taken place and were amazed that their friend could walk without discomfort or pain! It was my first breakthrough to seeing people touched and healed by the power of God. It truly boosted my faith to continue to pray for those who were sick.

I later prayed for a man who had been on disability for several years because of a cyst in his knee. His knee was swollen and he had difficulty with it for many years. As I prayed, I could feel the healing power of Jesus in my hands. The man exclaimed to me, "Your hands feel as if they were just taken out of a furnace!" The man later went to his doctor who took him off disability because the doctors could no longer find the cyst after performing an X-ray. He had been completely healed by the power of God!

I was invited around that time to preach in a little town in Indiana called Bedford. I prayed for a woman named Amanda who had had been diagnosed with scoliosis by the doctors when she was nine years of age. She'd had constant pain in her back and neck all her life. As I prayed for her, she said that she felt heat go into her neck and back. She went to work the next day and didn't feel any pain. I spoke with her a year later and she said that she was still healed by the power of God and hadn't experienced any symptoms of the condition since!

As I prayed for people, I would feel fire in my hands. I knew this to be a healing anointing that God had placed on my life to minister to the sick! Many times I can recognize when this anointing is in manifestation, just as others who operate in this same anointing can recognize this power. When the healing anointing comes, it feels like fire or even like electricity!

There is much we can learn as we study the life and healing ministry of Jesus! Let's take a look at the many methods and ways that Jesus ministered to the sick and how we can follow His example.

THE HEALING MINISTRY OF JESUS

We can glean a lot by observing the healing ministries of the past, especially if we follow after our greatest example of the healing ministry, Jesus! We know that Jesus had an earthly mission to go to the cross; yet, He was also given a special anointing to minister to the sick. As we take a look at His life and ministry, I want to emphasize the importance of understanding that Jesus didn't come to the earth to demonstrate healing or miracles as God. He came as our model and example to demonstrate what it was like to be a son *of* God, anointed *by* God. He didn't come to heal the sick because He was *God*. No, Jesus healed the sick because He was a *Man* anointed by God. Despite what some theologians would have you believe, Jesus never healed the sick out of His power or *deity* as being the second Person of the Trinity. The Bible clearly teaches us that Jesus laid aside His power as God when He came to the earth!

> *Who, being in the form of God, thought it not robbery to be equal with God: but made himself of no reputation, and took upon him the form of a servant, and was made in the likeness of men* (Philippians 2:6-7 KJV. See also Hebrews 10:5; 2:14,16).

Jesus was fully God and fully man. Yet, He laid aside His power as God to be anointed as a man in order to demonstrate the miraculous!

> *And Jesus, when he was baptized, went up straightway out of the water: and, lo, the heavens were opened unto him, and he saw the Spirit of God descending like a dove, and lighting upon him* (Matthew 3:16 KJV).

Jesus didn't begin His earthly ministry until *after* He was baptized by John, and the Holy Spirit came upon Him. The heavens opened and the glory came upon Him and *clothed* Him as if He were wrapped in a mantle! This was a divine commissioning that Jesus received from the Father! Jesus received the anointing in the same manner you and I do. He received it in same manner the 120 received the anointing in the upper room on the day of Pentecost! They were baptized into the person of the Holy Spirit and power came as a result!

> *How God anointed Jesus of Nazareth with the Holy Spirit and with power, who went about doing good **and***

healing all who were oppressed by the devil, for God was with Him (Acts 10:38).

Jesus was anointed and sent by God with a healing mantle! He was sent for the purpose of destroying the works of the devil! Sickness and disease is a work of the devil, as poverty and oppression over cities and regions is a work of the devil. Jesus came to wreak havoc on satan's kingdom by enforcing the will and dominion of His Father on the earth!

> *The Spirit of the Lord is upon Me, because He has anointed Me to preach the gospel to the poor; He has sent Me to heal the brokenhearted, to proclaim liberty to the captives and recovery of sight to the blind, to set at liberty those who are oppressed* (Luke 4:18).

At thirty years of age, Jesus began His healing ministry. Jesus knew that the anointing upon His life was for the purpose of releasing healing and deliverance to those bound by the enemy. Shortly after He began His ministry, His reputation began to spread because so many were healed and set free by the power of God's anointing!

> *Now a woman, having a flow of blood for twelve years, who had spent all her livelihood on physicians and could not be healed by any, came from behind and touched the border of His garment. And immediately her flow of blood stopped. And Jesus said, "Who touched Me?" When all denied it, Peter and those with him said, "Master, the multitudes throng and press You, and You say, 'Who touched Me?'" But Jesus said, "Somebody touched Me, for I perceived power going out from Me." Now when the woman saw that she was not hidden, she came trembling; and falling down before Him, she declared to Him in the presence of all the people the*

reason she had touched Him and how she was healed immediately (Luke 8:43-47).

This woman came seeking Jesus for healing, because she had heard of the works of Christ! She had heard of the healings that had taken place in other villages where Jesus had ministered. Faith rose up within her. She was determined that God would perform the miraculous in her life! As Jesus was walking through the crowd of people, the woman with the issue of blood pressed in through the crowd and grabbed hold of the hem of His garment. She was desperate to be healed of her condition. For twelve years she had suffered and given all her money to doctors, but she didn't get any better; in fact, she got worse. When she took hold of the hem of His garment, power was released! She placed a demand on the anointing, and healing power went through her body, and she was completely healed her of her condition. Jesus felt a release of that healing power. That's why the Bible records:

> *Jesus said, "Who touched Me?" When all denied it, Peter and those with him said, "Master, the multitudes throng and press You, and You say, 'Who touched Me?'" But Jesus said, "Somebody touched Me, for I perceived power going out from Me"* (Luke 8:45-46).

They must have been thinking, *What do you mean?* Jesus recognized the flow of the healing anointing. He knew what it felt like to have someone place a demand upon the anointing. Jesus turned to her and said, *"Daughter, your faith has made you well"* (Mark 5:34). Faith always places a demand on the anointing!

As we take a look at the eighth chapter of Luke, we can see that Jesus could feel and sense the release of the healing anointing. Jesus said He felt power go out of Him. He knew that the woman with the issue of blood had been completely healed! As we study how Jesus ministered to the sick, we can better understand how to minister and function in this particular call and better understand how to minister in this same anointing!

> *He who believes in Me...out of his heart will flow rivers of living water* (John 7:38).

We can compare the anointing to a flowing river! When the healing anointing is in manifestation, you can feel it flow from you as a rushing river. Over time, my wife and I have learned to be more sensitive to the healing anointing when it is in manifestation. For me, the healing anointing often comes in the form of fire on my shoulders or in my hands. It may even feel like electricity at times. I've even felt the mantle drip on me, on occasion. When I sense these things, I can often know the direction for the service!

I've noticed that when this anointing comes upon my wife, Amy, she will begin to receive words of knowledge that come to her in the form of seeing pictures. She may even receive the person's name and the illness they have been dealing with. As Amy and I were ministering in Kentucky at a three-day conference, my wife called out a word of knowledge for a woman who was having problems in her right knee from an injury. A woman came forward in response for the word, and Amy laid hands on her knee. The woman felt heat go into her knee, all the pain left and she was completely healed. The woman testified that she had an injury many years ago. She had fallen several feet through a porch and was unable to bend her knee for more than six years. Weeping, she knelt at the altar thanking God.

Hallelujah! Jesus' healing power set this woman free from six years of dealing with the mountain of impossibility that was in her life.

RETURNING TO THE FOUNDATION

As we study Jesus' life and ministry, we can see that He exudes a lifestyle of prayer and fasting. This is the lifestyle we are called to live if we expect to see the same results of power and manifestation that Jesus experienced in His earthly ministry! Not everyone has the same ministry or the same mantle. The mantle comes with the call! Yet, with every ministry we have a responsibility to steward the anointing that is upon our lives, and to know the purpose of the mantle that has been placed upon us.

Jesus was never without fresh oil! There will always be a need for fresh oil for the mantle. The secret place is the foundation upon which supernatural power, favor, and blessing continue. We must continually return to this foundation in order to see God's hand and power continually increase upon our lives! This is how we grow in the anointing that He has placed upon our lives.

I've often reminded myself of when the power of God first came on my life, when the favor of God first came on my life. It was when I encountered His glory in the secret place. We must continually return to this foundation. The power that we portray is a direct indication of our own individual prayer lives. Though we may have a mantle for healing, we are still reliant upon a fresh touch of the anointing to minister out of that mantle. When the anointing is not fresh upon our lives, then we fail to bring the same results we once did.

There will be times when we must draw away in fellowship and intimacy, just as Jesus did during His ministry. We can see the revelation of the secret place was prevalent in Jesus' ministry. Jesus remains as our greatest example of a role model. Especially as a five-fold ministry gift. He was the first Son of God; and as the Son of God, He practiced a lifestyle of prayer and fasting. His lifestyle was that of fellowship and intimacy with the Father in the secret place:

...He went out to the mountain to pray, and continued
all night in prayer to God (Luke 6:12).

This was the key that caused Jesus to see the multitudes healed! So much happens out of the overflow of the anointing in our lives; as we learn to minister out of the place of overflow, we will experience healings and miracles that we could have never thought possible!

When we are carriers of His presence, the lost are drawn to Jesus through us. This is what the Bible calls the ministry of reconciliation! So often I've found that when others are touched and healed by God, salvation becomes so easy for them to receive! I've seen many people healed in malls and grocery stores and then they become so willing to come to salvation!

PLANTING A SEED

I was in Wyoming ministering at a conference and my host asked me if I would like to minister on the Native American Reservation. I love ministering to the First Nations people. They are so sensitive to the power of God and open to the Holy Spirit. Many ministry people were too afraid to go to this reservation, but I told my host that I would love to minister there. They took me to a house where I ministered to an entire family. The owner of the house said to me, "There is a witch coven across the street, and they are tossing potions over my fence and causing demons to come into my house." As I prayed over the home, the glory of God began to fill the place. Then I began ministering to the family one by one. The Lord began to release His healing power and heal them.

There was a young man they wanted me to pray for; they told me that he had been strung out on drugs for many years. As I prayed for him, the power of God hit him and he began to weep in front of his whole family, saying, "I can feel the hand of God upon me." I could tell the Lord was moving on him in a powerful way. As this was happening, the boy's mother stormed out of the house. I later found out that she was part of the witch coven across the street.

I would like to say that this young man gave his life to the Lord that day, but sometimes we are sent by God just to plant a seed into someone's life. An encounter with the Holy Spirit is much like a seed being planted. They may come to the Lord as they are laying on their bed at night! They may forget a message they heard in church years ago. Yet, they will never forget a genuine encounter with the Holy Spirit!

Once, I was on my way to a mall with a few friends of mine. I felt like the Lord wanted me to talk to this young girl sitting outside a bookstore at the entrance of the mall. At first, I hesitated because she was with some of her friends. Still, I approached her and her friends and said, "Hi, I have a gift that causes people to feel a supernatural energy. When I pray to release that energy, people can become healed or they can feel that energy in their body."

The girl's friends began to laugh, but she agreed to let me pray for her. As I did, the power of God overcame her, and suddenly her friends began to pay attention. I then began to prophesy about some things going on in her life that only she and God knew. She was blown away. Then I said, "The energy that you felt is Jesus, and I just want you to know that He loves and cares about your life. Would you like to receive Jesus into your life?" She then said, "Thank you for praying for me; that really means a lot. But I still struggle with the idea that Jesus is the only way to Heaven."

I could tell that she had been touched by God and was still fighting it. Yet, I knew that it was a seed planted in her life and she will never forget the encounter that she had that day. I have seen so many come to salvation by simply bringing others into an encounter with the Holy Spirit. I always felt that arguing people into the Kingdom is a waste of time. We need to allow the Holy Spirit to woo and draw others to the

Father! Sometimes people are more than willing to receive Christ, and sometimes it's simply a seed planted in their heart. Just showing the world that God cares can be enough to drive the darkness away long enough for them to see the light! I truly feel that if we can keep showing people love, then eventually they will come to the Father!

THE IMPORTANCE OF PRAYER AND FASTING

One of the greatest revivalists we can look back on is Charles Finney. I remember reading once that he said if he ever felt the anointing begin to wane upon his life, he would immediately begin a three-day fast! We must be willing and dedicated to see the harvest come in, no matter the sacrifice or cost for God's precious anointing!

> *When they had come to the multitude, a man came to Him, kneeling down to Him and saying, "Lord, have mercy on my son, for he is an epileptic and suffers severely; for he often falls into the fire and often into the water. So I brought him to Your disciples, but they could not cure him." Then Jesus answered and said, "O faithless and perverse generation, how long shall I be with you? How long shall I bear with you? Bring him here to Me." And Jesus rebuked the demon, and it came out of him; and the child was cured from that very hour. Then the disciples came to Jesus privately and said, "Why could we not cast it out?" So Jesus said to them, "Because of your unbelief; for assuredly, I say to you, if you have faith as a mustard seed, you will say to this mountain, 'Move from here to there,' and it will move; and nothing will be impossible for you. However, this kind does not go out except by prayer and fasting* (Matthew 17:14-21).

The lifestyle that Jesus practiced was one of dedicated prayer and fasting. Jesus was always trying to get His disciples to adapt the same lifestyle as His, in order to cause their faith to reach the level of His faith. Jesus rebuked His disciples because it was possible for them to do what was asked of them by the man with a son suffering as an epileptic. This man longed to see his son set free from epileptic seizures, yet Jesus' disciples lacked the fresh anointing necessary to cast the demon out.

The power that we have operated in previously can be lacking in the present, because we have failed to receive the fresh touch of God upon our lives. The responsibility truly is on us to show the power of the risen Savior and what He can do for others faced with tragic impossibilities. God is willing and able to use us as vessels to release His miracles, signs, and wonders! There is something about fasting and prayer combined that brings an intensity of the anointing; it brings a freshness upon our lives! When the opportunity suddenly presents itself, we are loaded and ready—hallelujah!

Just as Jesus was present with His disciples, challenging them to reach to the highest heights of faith, Jesus is still speaking to us. Jesus is the Word; the Word and Christ are one. The Word is always speaking to us, challenging us, and calling us to that next level of commitment, that next level of faith! When we have come to the place where the Word does not challenge us, then we have stopped growing. We should continually allow the Word to challenge us in all areas of our faith so that we can grow and mature in the Lord!

AUTHORITY AND POWER

Then He called His twelve disciples together and gave them power and authority over all demons, and to cure diseases. He sent them to preach the kingdom of God and to heal the sick (Luke 9:1-2).

The two most commonly used words in the New Testament for power are the words *exousia* and *dunamis*. Jesus says in Acts 1:

> *But you shall receive* **power** *when the Holy Spirit has come upon you; and you shall be witnesses to Me in Jerusalem, and in all Judea and Samaria, and to the end of the earth* (Acts 1:8).

The word "power" in this portion of Scripture is the word *dunamis*, which means miraculous power, explosive power, even like dynamite! The anointing is like dynamite, explosive power. When it is in manifestation you can feel the anointing like a rushing river or in the form of burning fire! Authority is much different when it is in operation. You do not necessarily *feel* anything when you are stepping out in your God-given authority!

Authority is translated as *exousia,* which means a right, influence, or delegated right. Authority is much like faith in the sense that you do not feel any particular manifestation of the anointing, but you are using the faith and authority given by God to perform! Notice that Jesus sent them out with power and authority. He not only gave them power but also authority! It's equally important that we understand how to operate in authority, as well as power. It's not that the one is greater than the other. There will be times where we will be able to walk in both simultaneously. There will be times that *dunamis* power may not be in manifestation, and we will be forced to operate in authority, rather than the anointing. Part of what makes up our DNA as sons and daughters of God is the ability to walk in dominion and authority! We have authority over sickness, diseases, and over all demonic power.

Jesus operated out of both authority and power! Jesus not only healed the sick, but also cast out devils. The healing anointing is given not only for the purpose of healing those with sickness and disease, but also to cast out devils! There are demons that try to bring sickness upon people; that is not to say that everyone that has a physical ailment has a demon. Yet it's important to understand that demons are trespassers by nature, and they try to bring sickness upon those in the world and try to oppress believers with sickness as well. That is why it is so imperative that we understand our authority in God and take authority over them!

> *And there was a woman who for eighteen years had had an illness caused by a spirit (demon). She was bent double, and could not straighten up at all. When Jesus saw her, He called her over and said to her, "Woman, you are released from your illness." Then He laid His hands on her, and immediately she stood erect again and she began glorifying and praising God* (Luke 13:11-13 AMP).

This woman had suffered eighteen years with a spirit of infirmity. Yet, when Jesus prayed for her, the spirit left her and she was healed!

My wife and I were ministering together in Atlanta a few years ago. There was a powerful anointing released in those meetings. There were many who received healing and life-changing impartation! In those meetings, there were several deliverances that had taken place. A young woman approached my wife and I, explaining that for several years she had had stomach trouble and severe migraines. As we began to pray for her, the Lord revealed to me that this was caused by a spirit of infirmity. We took authority over the spirit and ministered the anointing to her. The next day she came to us and said that she had slept peacefully for the first time in many years! Her stomach was healed, and she was no longer experiencing any migraines!

> *There was a man in the synagogue who was possessed by the spirit of an unclean demon; and he cried out with a loud and terrible voice, "Let us alone! What business do we have [in common] with each other, Jesus of Nazareth?*

Have You come to destroy us? I know who You are—the Holy One of God!" But Jesus rebuked him, saying, "Be silent (muzzled, gagged) and come out of him!" And when the demon had thrown the man down among them, he came out of him without injuring him in any way. They were all astonished and in awe, and began saying to one another, "What is this message? For with authority and power He commands the unclean spirits and they come out!" (Luke 4:33-36 AMP)

Jesus exercised authority and power many times when dealing with devils! He operated in both authority and power as the Son of God! So many were impressed by Jesus, because up until that time, no one had the ability to cast out devils. Jesus was a brand-new model! A new representation of the Son of God with power and authority!

As we study the ministry of Jesus, we can see that He didn't always minister to the sick in the same way, there were many ways that He ministered to those in need. There were times when Jesus ministered to the sick out of the anointing, other times out of authority, and sometimes both! It's not necessarily true that one way of ministering is greater than the other, so long as we are bearing fruit and reaching success!

Amy and I were ministering in a church in Milwaukee, Wisconsin. During the conference, the Lord healed a woman who was in need of a new rotator cuff as she was unable to lift up her arm. The Lord gave her a healing that night and she received full mobility! Some of the greatest healings and miracles my wife and I have seen in our ministry have happened through radical faith.

There have been times when we have prayed in faith and felt nothing, but God would perform the most notable miracles! The pastor asked us to pray for a woman who had stage-four cancer. She had eight brain tumors and was given only six weeks to live. As my wife and I prayed, we spoke by faith and commanded the tumors to die. Our friend, Pastor Jaye Jaye, later told us that God had performed a miracle—the eight brain tumors could not be found!

We have learned that there are many different ways we can minister to the sick: through the laying on of hands, through ministering the healing anointing, as well as through ministering by faith and authority alone to see the others healed, set free, and delivered. We may not see all healed through the anointing alone. It's so important that we learn to minister healing and deliverance in many different ways!

ENDNOTES

1. Kenneth E. Hagin, *The Holy Spirit and His Gifts* (Kenneth Hagin Ministries, 1991).
2. http://en.believethesign.com/index.php/William_Branham#cite_note-51; accessed August 28, 2018.
3. Lester Sumrall, *The Gifts and Ministries of the Holy Spirit* (New Kensington, PA: Whitaker House, 2005).
4. Lester Sumrall, *Pioneers of Faith* (Tulsa, OK: Harrison House, 1995).
5. T.L. Osborn on Branham, YouTube; accessed June 13, 2018.
6. Randy Clark and Bill Johnson, *Anointed to Heal* (Grand Rapids, MI: Chosen Books).

CHAPTER 3

HEALING AND MIRACLE MANTLES FROM THE PAST

by Jesse

There are so many great evangelists, harvesters, and miracles workers who made a significant impact in their day and saw a great harvest of souls come in! Their stories should never be forgotten, but instead passed on throughout the generations. As they have gone on to be with the Lord, it's as if the baton has been passed from one generation to another, and it's time for another generation to begin to rise up and run the race!

I believe that now, in this significant hour of church history, God is looking to release mantles upon a new generation; it's time for an army of miracle workers to arise, to usher in the harvest! What we are seeing is a merging of the generations, like a new wineskin being built as

God joins the Joshuas and Calebs together for the purpose of advancing His Kingdom on the earth. This is a generation that will carry the new wine, the fragrance of Christ's anointing throughout the world!

Let us look back upon the mantles of old, those mantles that God placed upon great men and women. Let's not think in our minds, *It's great what God did in that time, or era.* Rather, let us think, *Lord, we are excited for what You have yet to do, and what You have yet to release in this hour, in this generation!*

There are many great men and women I could mention in this chapter who have pushed beyond the limits of what was considered normal in their day. Such great sacrifices were made, tied to great persecution. They are what we call pioneers, those whose legacies have carried on as a flame that has been deposited within the next generation to burn, to go beyond what they have accomplished, calling others to press in to greater things!

JOHN ALEXANDER DOWIE[1]

One of the greatest pioneers in the healing ministry we can look back on today is John Alexander Dowie. When Dowie was beginning his journey into ministry, he began pastoring a church in Sydney, Australia. Suddenly, a plague struck Australia and brought great devastation with it! Many of his own congregation died from this plague. Dowie saw forty members of his own congregation buried in just a matter of weeks. As he began to study the verse, Acts 10:38 became more real to John Dowie than ever before. It was a revelation that he had received!

> *How God anointed Jesus of Nazareth with the Holy Ghost and with power; who went about doing good, and healing all that were oppressed of the devil; for God was with him* (Acts 10:38 KJV).

Dowie suddenly realized the cure: Jesus was the healer! The revelation must have dawned on him that God was with him, just as God was with Jesus to heal the sick! He later received word that another woman, who was part of his congregation no less, was dying due to the plague. Dowie rushed to the hospital and proclaimed that she would live! The woman was completely healed, and this was the beginning of John Alexander Dowie's healing ministry! I feel that his ministry was apostolic in nature. Dowie founded Zion, Illinois, a city built and cultivated by the miraculous! His pioneering spirit and mantle caused him to birth a city that was established by healings and miracles! He placed wheelchairs, canes, and braces upon the wall of his church, Zion Tabernacle, that filled 6,000 per service! It is believed that more than one million were converted to Christianity through his ministry!

Dowie took such a militant stance on divine healing that he was placed behind bars on several occasions, accused of practicing medicine without a license on a hundred occasions. As Dowie was preaching in Chicago, he suddenly began to prophesy. He prophesied the invention of television on October 16, 1904, saying:

> I know the possibilities of electricity. It is possible that it may yet convey the face of the speaker, and by photoelectricity, show the man as he is talking. Perhaps a discourse delivered here may be heard in every city of the United States. Some day that will be so and the word spoken in Shiloh Tabernacle will be heard even in the furthest corners of the earth.

On September 5, 1897, John Dowie prophesied the invention of the radio in a meeting in Chicago. He prophesied that the voice of an individual would be carried through the radio into other cities and regions! We honor men like John Alexander Dowie and we would call him a true pioneer, as he was the first to blaze the trail and break through into the supernatural in a way that few have!

Dowie had such fire, zeal, and passion to see the miraculous! We can see that the flame that had burned so brightly in Dowie began to burn even brighter in a man named John G. Lake. That is what is so powerful about impartation; the very same anointing can be transferred from one life to another!

We should value impartation above everything else in our lives and ministries. Impartation has been practiced since the early church and we need it today. Especially by those who have already been where we desire to go and what we so desperately long to see in God! All it takes is one impartation to change everything for your destiny. We can certainly see the evidence of the power of impartation in John G. Lake's ministry!

JOHN G. LAKE

In the life of John G. Lake, we can see the torch of impartation that passed from one generation to another. John Alexander Dowie seemed in a way to be John G. Lake's Elijah. We can see an even greater portion of the anointing in Lake's life, as he received from the passing of the mantle that was on Dowie. John G. Lake was raised with fifteen brothers and sisters. So much sorrow filled his childhood, and he recalls empty memories filled with hospitals and graveyards. He lost eight of his brothers to disease.

Later in life, Lake married and his wife became sick. The doctors pronounced her condition to be incurable. After Lake received news of John Dowie's ministry of healing, he decided it would be best to have his wife prayed for by John Dowie. His wife was completely healed! Later, Lake brought his brother and two sisters to Dowie to be healed![2]

John G. Lake wrote, "We took our dying brother to a Healing Home in Chicago, where prayer was offered for him with the laying on of hands. He received an instant healing and arose from the death bed a well man."[3]

Lake was greatly impacted by John Alexander Dowie in many different parts of his life. He was immediately thrust into the healing ministry. By examining his childhood, we can see why Lake was so fierce and bold through his ministry when dealing with sickness and disease. He had a compassion burning in him to see people healed and set free as he witnessed other members of his family healed.

Later, Lake began his ministry in Spokane, Washington, by establishing healing rooms, a model that originated with his mentor, John Dowie. Lake wrote that God had taken him to Spokane where he ministered to hundreds of sick people every week. People came from as far as 5,000 miles away for healing. God graciously answered their call for healing.[4] During the time that John G. Lake was in Spokane, it was documented that over 100,000 healings had taken place in only five to six years. At that time Spokane was declared to be the healthiest city in America.[5]

> Since the establishment of the Spokane Divine Healing Institution in January 1915, Spokane has become the healthiest city in the United States, according to the national record. and Dr. Rutledge of Washington, D.C., in reviewing this subject said, Divine healing is no longer a vagary [irrational or unpredictable idea] to be smiled at. Through its practise, the Divine Healing Institute of Spokane, Reverend John G. Lake, Overseer, has made Spokane the healthiest city in the United States, In this I do not discount all the other splendid agencies of healing, but I call attention to the fact that with the establishing of Divine Healing Institute of Spokane, the percentage of deaths in the city was

lowered to that extent that Spokane became famed as the healthiest city in the United States of America.[6]

Lake also greatly impacted the city of Portland, Oregon. It's clear to see the mantle that was on his life was apostolic and greatly impacted the Pacific Northwest.

When John G. Lake felt the leading of the Lord to go to South Africa, he brought a team of people with him. The team arrived only to find that a plague had ravaged South Africa and that people were dying almost quicker than men could dig the graves. Lake and his team volunteered to help bury the bodies. Doctors began to take notice that Lake was not contracting the disease. Lake agreed to have a doctor perform a test on him to study. The scientist took a germ from one of the victims of the bubonic plague and placed it upon John G. Lakes hand. To the doctors' amazement, they found that the plague had died on his hand. When he was asked how this was possible, Lake's response:

> It is the law of the Spirit of Life in Christ Jesus, I believe that just as long as I keep my soul in contact with the living God so that His Spirit is flowing into my soul and body, that no germ will ever attach itself to me, for the Spirit of God will kill it.[7]

I personally feel that John G. Lake stands as one of the greatest generals, not only for the great exploits that followed his ministry, but due to the fact that he carried such in-depth revelation of the Word of God. I feel the body of Christ could greatly benefit from the revelation that he carried! His legacy continues to light fires in the hearts of evangelists, miracle workers, and harvesters throughout the generations. I've always enjoyed the thought that the cloud of witnesses is cheering us on in the race (see Heb. 12:1). It's time for another generation to lay hold of the torch of revival and spread the fire!

MARIA WOODWORTH ETTER

Maria Woodworth Etter was born in Lisbon, Columbiana, Ohio. What she wrote about her childhood was very sorrowful. She remembered her family being very poor. One of the tragedies in her life was the sudden loss of her father. She remarks in her diary that "I am a drunkard's daughter, with all the other dark trials to go through. I have never given this to the public before, but feel led of God to let the world know how the Lord called and lifted me out of the depths."[8]

Etter recalls living with her mother and eight sisters after the loss of her father. She spoke of being converted and filled with the Spirit at age thirteen.

> At the age of thirteen I attended a meeting of the Disciples Church. My family were all Disciples, at this time. When I heard the story of the cross, my heart was filled with the love of Jesus. My eyes seemed to be fountains of tears.[9]

Etter felt the call to preach the gospel at an early age, but refused the responsibility. She was later married and had six children; however, five of the children died due to disease, leaving only her oldest, Elizabeth.[10]

One day Etter had a prophetic encounter; the Lord brought her into a vision:

> Angels came into her room. They took her to the West, over prairies, lakes, forest, and rivers where she saw a long, wide field of waving golden grain. As the view unfolded, she began to preach and saw the grains begin to fall like sheaves. Then Jesus told her that, just as the grain fell, so people would fall as she preached.[11]

Such a powerful mantle rested upon the life of Etter. She is a general in her own right and held the scars to prove it. She was a forerunner who bravely obeyed the call of God when there was great persecution attached to being a woman preacher.

> St. Louis, Missouri - rejoice with us in the goodness of our God and Saviour, for He has been very gracious to us. During the last two months, at Sister Woodworth-Etter's meetings alone, hundreds have been saved, and a greater number healed. Most of the latter were chronic cases; many only came after the doctors had pronounced them incurable. One woman had spent $500 on her child for healing. Several hundred have had hearing restored; some had been paralyzed, others had tumors, consumption, and withered limbs, and were healed.[12]

There was a powerful glory resting on Maria Woodworth Etter's life. Unusual manifestation accompanied her ministry. For example, people from miles away fell into trances and would have visions of Heaven and hell, and when many would come out of these trances, they would become converted. She wrote, "For twenty miles around men and woman were struck down in their homes, in business places, and on the roads and streets. Some lay for hours and had wonderful visions."[13]

> When she ministered, the power of God often came upon her. Once she stood with her mouth open and her hand up, about to make a point, for three days and three nights. She never moved. For those three days and nights all of her physical functions ceased; she didn't eat any food or drink any water. Naturally, anybody caught up in all that glory could go without food, water, or anything.
>
> —KENNETH E. HAGIN,
> *A Common Sense Guide to Fasting*

John G. Lake was impressed by Maria Woodworth Etter and the signs and wonders that accompanied her ministry. He referred to her as "Mother Etter." She was also an inspiration to and greatly impacted Aimee Semple McPherson's ministry.[14]

Maria Woodworth Etter was a voice that God raised up. She was a forerunner for the miraculous! The testimony of her life is such that it speaks of the possibility that anyone can be a sign and a wonder for their generation! She faced all the persecution and opposition that came against her destiny and calling. The story of her life speaks of an overcomer! It's time for another generation of women to arise into the miraculous!

KENNETH HAGIN

Many of the healing evangelists of the past that we know of today were derived from what is known as the healing revival of the 1950s. Kenneth Hagin's ministry was not on the forefront during this time. Some even criticized him for not being on the cutting edge, yet in the later years of his life, we see that God had placed something in him to impart not only to his generation, but to future generations.

Kenneth Hagin began his ministry as a Baptist minister, but he later ventured out into the healing ministry, eventually becoming the leader of the "Word of Faith" movement. What God placed in him was bigger than just a single era or generation. The wisdom he walked in was well ahead of his time. Hagin understood the importance of the healing ministry, as he saw incredible healings and miracles birthed through his ministry. Hagin brought wisdom not only to his generation, but to forthcoming generations. He understood that we could see greater results in healing if we were able to combine ministering out of the healing anointing, coupled with the word of knowledge and praying out of simple faith in the Word of God.

The Lord Jesus appeared to Kenneth Hagin and placed in him a special anointing to minister.

> I remember something that Jesus said to me when He appeared to me in that first vision in 1950 in Rockwall, Texas. After Jesus laid the finger of His right hand in the palm of each one of my hands and they began to burn just like I was holding a coil of fire, He said to me, "Kneel down before Me." I knelt down before Him, and He laid His hand on my hand and said, "I have called thee and have anointed thee and have given unto thee a special anointing to minister to the sick."[15]

There are those who are anointed with a special anointing to minister to sick. Throughout church history we have evidence of that.

KATHRYN KUHLMAN

Something that has always stirred the flame in my heart is studying the lives of the past revivalists, reading about the generals, and how God used them. They were just ordinary people who were hungry for God, and they pressed in until they received something from Heaven—an anointing or a special mantle in order to set a generation on fire! As I have studied the lives of the generals, I have often hoped and dreamed that God would use me in a similar way, and possibly you have as well. They are examples of what ordinary people have become through desperate hunger.

Something we can say that every great man or woman of God had in common was that they all had devoted prayer lives. They lived a lifestyle of prayer and fasting. They lived surrendered lives, yielded to the hand of God that rested upon them.

*His brightness is like the sunlight; He has [bright] rays
flashing from His hand, and there [in the sunlike splen-
dor] is the hiding place of His power* (Habakkuk 3:4
AMP).

Another of the generals we can glean from is Kathryn Kuhlman.
She knew that the hiding place of God's power was sought and found
through divine intimacy, divine fellowship with the Holy Spirit. One
of the greatest revelations that Kuhlman possessed was of the favor and
power that comes as a result of true fellowship and friendship with the
Holy Spirit.

I once read that Kathryn Kuhlman was in a miracle service. So
many had received miracles, with canes, braces and empty wheelchairs
behind her. She stood boldly on the platform and pointed to a group of
preachers and said, "Any one of you can have this anointing that is on
my life, if you will just pay the price." She often spoke of the price that
she paid for the anointing that was on her life. She once said referring to
the anointing, "It costs much, but it is worth the price." Though I never
had the privilege of attending one of her meetings, it is plain to see that
she was an example for so many of those that desire to see God's power
as she did! She had a revelation of the vital importance of prayer and the
power that it produces.

The key to Kathryn Kuhlman's ministry was her desire to spend
time in the secret place! It is the price of being a friend of God! There
is a price to the anointing. One of the keys that we can take from her
ministry is this: she understood the key to the tangible power of God.
Her ministry was birthed from her own personal prayer life. It was her
fellowship and intimacy with God that caused an overflow of miracles
to take place in her meetings.

Those who personally knew Kuhlman noticed that she would often
wait for the manifest presence of Jesus to come into her meetings before

she would even walk upon the platform to minister. She loved to minister out of the glory of God, or as a better way of saying it, the manifest presence of Jesus Christ. One time when leaving a miracle service, as she was walking through the kitchen of the hotel, the staff of the hotel began to fall out under the power of God. There was something so powerful, so tangible that rested on her life.

MIRACLE-WORKING POWER

God has used many people so mightily throughout the years of church history, those we can look back on and glean from to help us better understand our own individual calling or function as members of the body of Christ. These great men and women who were so powerfully used by God in the past have become our models, our examples of what we can obtain in God and in the miraculous. They have made a significant impact upon generations. They made their mark and later earned the status of being "generals." As we study their lives, they challenge us to step into greater boldness and higher levels of the anointing by following in their footsteps. Many of them have indefinitely raised the bar for the miraculous.

There is so much that we can learn by observing their anointings and functions in the body of Christ. I believe it's best to glean from how God used them from behind the pulpit, rather than focus on the shortcomings in their personal lives. Perhaps God has called you to have a similar ministry or mantle as some of the generals mentioned in this book.

I feel that it's important we remember these men and women who carved a path into the supernatural and pushed the limits. If we are to expect the same measure of power that they operated in, we must journey down the same path. They paid a great price for the anointing, as should we. Let's continue to examine the price that they paid and what it was that caused the anointing to rest so mightily upon their lives.

A.A. ALLEN

A.A. Allen said, "The student of Jesus Christ cannot become greater than his teacher. He cannot learn anything which Jesus did not know. He cannot find a shortcut to power with God. If he should try it, he will only meet with disappointment and sorrow."[16]

Now I want to focus your attention on A.A. Allen's ministry, because there was something so rare and so unique about the mantle that God had placed on his life. During the healing revival in the 1950s, Allen was one of the forerunners. During this time there were so many who were commissioned and hand selected by God into the healing ministry. God called them to take a gift of healing around the world! Allen had something different. What separates Allen from so many was that he not only had a healing mantle like so many others, but Allen had a special anointing for miracles, signs, and wonders.

> It was while pastoring my first church, an Assembly of God church in Colorado, that I definitely made up my mind that I must hear from heaven, and know the reason that my ministry was not confirmed by signs and wonders... I felt that if I would fast and pray, God would in some way speak to me, and reveal to me what stood between me and the miracle-working power of Jesus.[17]

Allen desperately wanted to see the power of God in the way that the apostles did in the Bible, and he was willing to pay any price for it. Allen told his wife, Lexie, to lock him inside his prayer closet and not open the door until he heard from Heaven. There were many times that he would enter his closet to pray and fast and begin knocking on the door because he could smell a meal being prepared by his wife. One day, his wife let him out of the closet; and as he sat to eat the meal and took just one bite, he arose from the table and told his wife once again to lock him in the closet and not open the door until he had the answer. He refused to give up until he had the key to operating in miracle-working power.

One day, suddenly a light began to shine in the closet, and he thought to himself that maybe it was his wife opening the door. Instead, God's glory came rushing in. Allen described his visitation from the Lord as a door that opened up for him in Heaven. Light and power began to fill his closet to the point that Allen thought he might die because of the power of God's glory permeating his body. The Lord then spoke to Allen and gave him a list of requirements that he was to perform in order to see the miracle-working power of Jesus in his life and ministry. After given the list, the Lord then spoke to Allen and said, "You will not only heal the sick, but you shall cast out devils and see mighty miracles in My name."

A.A. Allen received a mantle for miracles during his visitation in his prayer closet. Something was placed on his life—it was miraculous power!

NOTABLE MIRACLES

Few have operated in a level of miraculous power the way A.A. Allen did throughout his ministry. R.W. Schambach, a spiritual son of Allen's, recalls one of the most notable miracles that took place in A.A. Allen's ministry:

> A woman brought her child, who had twenty-six major diseases, to our meeting. I'll never forget this as long as I live. The boy was born blind, deaf, and mute. Both arms were crippled and deformed. His elbows protruded up

into his little tummy; his knees touched his elbows. Both legs were crippled and deformed; he had club feet... Allen said, "I'm being carried away in the Spirit..." That night he said, "I'm being carried away to a huge building. Oh, it's a hospital..." Then he said, "I'm inside the hospital, and there's no doubt in my mind where I'm heading because I hear all the babies crying..." Brother Allen continued, "Twenty-six diseases. The doctors said he'd never live to see his first birthday, but that's not so. That boy is approaching four. Now I see the mother packing a suitcase. They're driving down the highway. I see the Alabama/Tennessee border. That automobile is driving in the parking lot. Lady, you're here tonight. Bring me that baby! God's going to give you twenty-six miracles." That lady came running... She put the baby in brother A.A. Allen's arms. That little boy's tongue had been hanging out of his mouth all week.

The first thing I saw as Brother Allen prayed was that tongue snap back in the mouth like a rubber band... I saw brand-new brown eyes. Then those little arms began to snap like pieces of wood; and for the first time, they stretched out. The legs cracked like wood popping. All of a sudden, I saw God form toes out of those club feet as easily as a child forms something with silly putty... This miracle charged up the people of God so much that even more miracles began to happen there in Birmingham... When everybody saw the power of God at work, all the handicapped people in wheelchairs stood up like a platoon of soldiers and walked out of there healed by the power of God.[18]

Schambach said that Allen would see the greatest miracles when he would fast. Many times, Allen would fast only water when he was ministering.[19]

Allen not only saw notable remarkable miracles, but he also saw supernatural signs and wonders such as oil coming out of people's hands.[20]

Schambach served for many years under Allen during the Voice of Healing, until he went on to have a great evangelistic ministry himself. For many years, R.W. Schambach saw incredible, notable miracles similar to those Allen performed by God's power. R.W. Schambach was incredibly impacted through Allen's ministry, but he wasn't the only one to come out of his ministry. There was a young man named Leroy Jenkins who was incredibly imparted too through Allen's ministry.

THE MIRACLE ARM

Leroy Jenkins had attended one of Allen's tent meetings. The man had severely injured his arm by trying to move a 250-pound section of plate glass. Leroy stated that the glass had severed through his muscle and also his bone; his arm was barely held together by his flesh. As he was brought to the hospital, the doctors suggested amputating the arm as they saw no chance of recovery. His arm was already turning black. As he refused to have his arm amputated, the doctors had no choice but to put his arm in a cast. Just a few days later, Jenkins went to A.A. Allen's tent revival. Everyone attending the meeting saw Leroy take off the cast and raise his arm in the air, completely healed!

Jenkins said, "I stretched it out and looked at my fingers. They were like those of a baby's hands. They were a different color and a different temperature. When I touched something with one finger, I felt it in all of the other fingers. It was so helpless, yet it was still alive."[21]

The miracle was later recorded in A.A. Allen's magazine. Leroy joined Allen as an associate and testified in his meetings of the miracle that he received in his arm. Later he went on to have his own evangelistic ministry, seeing the wheelchairs emptied and incurable diseases healed such as AIDS.

The fruit that came from Allen's ministry was evident. As his ministry went on through the years, he continued to press in for the miraculous and was not bothered by his critics. If anything, his critics caused him to want to answer their doubt with the undeniable proof of the miraculous power of Jesus that was prevalent in his ministry. He still stands as one of the greatest examples of someone who paid the price for God's miracle-working power!

WILLIAM BRANHAM

William Branham was born in extreme poverty in a little cabin in the backwoods of Kentucky. His parents recalled a supernatural occurrence that took place at his birth in that little cabin. From the time he was born, his life was marked by signs and wonders. Throughout his life he had several visitations with the angel of Lord, as well as the Lord Jesus!

During one such visitation that Branham received, the angel of the Lord told him, "I am sent from the presence of Almighty God to you that your peculiar birth and misunderstood life has been to indicate that you are to take a gift of divine healing to the peoples of the world. If you will be sincere when you pray and can get the people to believe you, nothing shall stand before your prayer, not even cancer."[22]

The angel also told him that he would be able to detect the diseases in people's bodies when this gift was in manifestation! It was that visitation on May 7, 1946, that launched Branham into full-time ministry and caused him to take a gift of divine healing around the world. Branham became a forerunner of the 1950s healing revival. He was the first to preach in large auditoriums and tents, ministering divine healing! There were many who went on to preach under the great white tents, but Branham was the first. Many gleaned from his ministry and were greatly influenced by him, such as Oral Roberts, T.L. Osborn, A.A. Allen, and many others.

William Branham inspired an entire generation to move in miracles, signs, and wonders! Though he was not an educated man, or a great orator, there is much to be said about the Prophet William Branham. His ministry impacted thousands upon thousands across the globe!

LONNIE FRISBEE

To sum up Lonnie's story in a few words: God got hold of a young radical hippie who ignited a fire within a generation to burn for Jesus. Lonnie was a true gift to the body of Christ. The presence of Jesus on his life drove thousands upon thousands to the Lord. What was on Lonnie's life was a mantle for power evangelism! What he carried was something special and unique that drew people to the manifest presence of Jesus!

At the age of eighteen, Lonnie had an encounter with the Lord that changed his life forever. He was a lost hippie kid bound on drugs searching for truth. One day he went to one of his favorite spots, the Tahquitz Canyon Trail in Southern California. Lonnie writes in *Not by Might Nor By Power, The Jesus Revolution, Volume 1:*

> I took all my clothes off and literally screamed up to heaven, "Jesus, if you are really real...reveal yourself to me!" Suddenly the atmosphere began to change around me. I knew that I was in the presence of God Almighty. Then I saw a radiant vision, clear as crystal. I saw thousands and thousands of young people at the ocean lined up in huge crowds along the coast, going out into the water to be baptized. I could see it! I knew instantly

that Jesus was real and that he was calling me to follow him. As the Lord lifted up my eyes. I saw a harvest field of people. They were like a huge wheat field. I saw in the vision thousands of people in the valley of decision.[22]

Throughout the years, Lonnie saw the vision slowly unfold before his eyes. The vision was slowly becoming a reality. Lonnie began preaching at a Calvary Chapel church in Southern California. In a church that seated over a thousand, it suddenly became packed out from wall to wall with young hippies.

We were leading hundreds of hippies and young people to the Lord on the beaches, in our communities, in church, in bible studies, in restaurants, at concerts, and just about everywhere. The electrifying atmosphere is so hard to capture into words. It was tangible.[23]

Lonnie had birthed a movement and it was growing rapidly. He never credited himself to be the only voice that influenced the Jesus Movement, but we can see the impact that Lonnie made upon a generation. He had sparked something and was making a tremendous impact!

Lonnie made mention of how Kathryn Kuhlman had such an impact on his life and ministry. He shared that one of his greatest joys was ministering with Kathryn: "For about seven years, I would go up to the Shrine Auditorium in Los Angeles each month to the Kathryn Kuhlman meetings. I witnessed undeniable miracles. The presence of the Holy Spirit would be so powerful that it overwhelmed me. I was drawn to those meetings like a magnet and longed for the gift of healing and miracles in my own life. ...Kathryn Kuhlman was definitely a wonderful spiritual mother and mentor to me. She had such a huge impact on my life. Before she died in 1976, she laid hands on me in a prayer of impartation."[24]

Lonnie believed in the power of impartation! It was only a few years later after Lonnie received his last impartation from Kathryn that the Vineyard Movement began! On Mother's Day, May 11, 1980, Lonnie was introduced by John Wimber to minister to his congregation. Lonnie ministered the word and shared his heart about revival. As they all began to worship the Lord, Lonnie called for all the young people, twenty-five years of age and younger, to come forward for prayer: "While they were still singing, I went into the crowd, laying hands on some of the young people. Kids were on the floor crying, shaking, speaking in tongues. Chairs went flying as people crashed into them. ...While people were singing one of my favorite songs, 'Hallelujah,' the Holy Spirit fell on the crowd in a fresh wave of power that was absolutely astounding.[25]

What began on Mother's Day turned into an outpouring of God's Spirit. What took place on this day launched the Vineyard Movement!

What I love about Lonnie's ministry was how he focused on the harvest, and as a result the outpouring came. Our focus should be the same! We should always be focused on the Great Commission and advancing God's Kingdom on earth. At the same time, we should position our hearts in such a way that we are open to the Lord releasing a fresh wave! Let us be careful not to miss it! Our prayer should be, "Lord, release a fresh move of Your Spirit for this time, for this generation. We are ready!"

We should honor these mantles from the past, although many times there was failure, and controversy. Still, there was also great success in advancing God's Kingdom on the earth!

These are just a few men and women who shook the earth! God is looking for more! There is something so intriguing about how God used men and women of faith such as Kenneth Hagin, William Branham,

Kathryn Kuhlman, and Maria Woodworth Etter. One thing they all had in common was that they all had devoted prayer lives!

I've always loved to study revival history to learn how revival fires shook nations, cities, and regions for God. There have been so many moves of God that we can talk about from the past, and even recent moves that have taken place that stir our hearts for believing God to release something new and fresh once again! It's in the heart of any believer: the desire to see a move of God that draws souls into His Kingdom. I truly believe that God releases sovereign outpourings and revivals. Yet, I also believe we can be intentional about bringing His Kingdom to earth.

I've noticed that so much of today's mindset in the church is that God is waiting for the right season or time to release revival. I would argue that God is waiting on His church to release revival! He desires to release Heaven on earth corporately as well as individually. Isn't that what revival is, Heaven coming to earth?

ENDNOTES

1. Content for the John Alexander Dowie section has been adapted from Roberts Liardon's, *John Alexander Dowie* (New Kensington, PA: Whitaker House, 1996), 26. And *The Miracle Ministry of the Prophet* by Christian Harfouche (Christian Pub., 1993), 14.

2. Roberts Liardon, *God's Generals* Video Series, John G. Lake: Man of God.

3. John G. Lake, *Diary of God's Generals* (Tulsa, OK: Harrison House, 2004).

4. John G. Lake, *Adventures in God*.

5. Healing rooms.com, *History of John G. Lake;* accessed June 15, 2018.

6. Roberts Liardon, *John G. Lake on Healing* (New Kensington, PA: Whitaker House, 2009), 27.

7. Liardon, *Diary of God's Generals.*

8. Maria Woodworth Etter, *Signs and Wonders* (New Kensington, PA: Whitaker House, 1997).

9. Ibid.

10. Rick Joyner, *Maria Woodworth Etter 1844-1924* (Morningstar ministries.org).

11. Liardon, *Diary of God's Generals.*

12. Etter, *Signs and Wonders.*

13. Ibid.

14. Joyner, *Maria Woodworth Etter 1844-1924;* Roberts Liardon, *Diary of God's Generals.*

15. Kenneth Hagin, *The Healing Anointing* (Broken Arrow, OK: Faith Library Publications, 1997).

16. A.A. Allen, *The Price of Miracle-Working Power of Jesus.*

17. R.W. Schambach, *You Can't Beat God-Givin'* (TBN Edition, 1994).

18. Robin Harfouche, *Miracles Today.*

19. Liardon, *Diary of God's Generals.*

20. Leroy Jenkins, *In the Presence of Mine Enemies* (Winters Publishing, 2013).

21. Owen Jorgensen, *Supernatural: The Life of William Branham* (Tucson Tabernacle, 1994).

22. Lonnie Frisbee with Roger Sachs, *Not By Might Nor By Power: The Jesus Revolution, Volume 1* (Middlebury, VT: Freedom Publications, 2012).

23. Ibid.

24. Ibid.

25. Lonnie Frisbee with Roger Sachs, *Not By Might Nor By Power: The Jesus Revolution, Volume 2* (Middlebury, VT: Freedom Publications, 2012).

CHAPTER 4

OUR JOURNEY
TOGETHER INTO
THE MIRACULOUS

by Jesse

When I first met my wife, Amy, and shook her hand, I can honestly tell you that I felt electricity flowing through my hand. It was spiritual, and I instantly knew that God was up to something. It was an instant connection. I knew that she was the one God had for me. I knew it was a confirmation to a word that my mother had given to me years ago. She told me the very year that I would meet my wife, and that we would travel and preach the gospel together. Amy was a confirmation to that word and prayer!

On our first date, Amy and I began to talk about our desire for ministry, to preach the gospel in other nations and win souls for Jesus. We were soon married and immediately began our ministry together!

It's been an incredible journey that we have experienced together over the years that we wouldn't trade for anything! We have seen God's favor and miraculous power as we have traveled in the U.S. as well as overseas together.

One of the revelations that God began to deposit in us early on in our ministry, was the importance of compassion and how healings and miracles are connected to compassion. One of the greatest verses that reveals the compassion of Christ is found in the gospel of Matthew.

> *When He saw the crowds, He was moved with compassion and pity for them, because they were dispirited and distressed, like sheep without a shepherd* (Matthew 9:36 AMP).

What I love about this verse is that it not only reveals the compassion of Christ, but the heart of the Father for the multitudes, for the lost and the broken.

As Jesus looked upon the multitudes, He saw the needs of the people, those who were lame, the deaf, the blind. He was moved with compassion. Something deep within the heart of Jesus was stirred for the multitudes; compassion rose up in Him like a fire. It was the love and mercy of God! He was moved, compelled to heal them. Jesus said, *"Most assuredly, I say to you, the Son can do nothing of Himself, but what He sees the Father do; for whatever He does, the Son also does in like manner"* (John 5:19). What did Jesus see His Father doing? He saw the desire of His Father to heal the brokenhearted, open the eyes of the blind, and to raise the dead. That is the will of our heavenly Father, for His Kingdom to come and for His will to be done (see Matt. 6:10). We have that same DNA, and that same nature that Jesus had in Him. Love is the very core of our makeup; we were created to be love and to walk in compassion.

*That Christ may dwell in your hearts through faith;
that you, being rooted and grounded in love, may be able
to comprehend with all the saints what is the width and
length and depth and height—to know the love of Christ
which passes knowledge; that you may be filled with all
the fullness of God* (Ephesians 3:17-19).

I love how Paul describes the love of God. He compares God's love to a mighty rushing river! Just as it is in the natural, a river can be felt and experienced. In the same way, God's love is tangible and passes our comprehension. It is an *experiential* knowledge. We can feel God's love and enter into the depths of the fire of His love! It sets our hearts ablaze! When we encounter the love of God, we are forever changed!

There is nothing I love more than seeing someone experience the love of God for the first time. It is priceless to see the expression on a person's face when the love of God suddenly goes beyond words, beyond a sermon, when the Holy Spirit moves on their hearts and tears begin to flow...they know that God loves them because they experienced Him! It is worth it all just to know that the person will never forget that moment, to know that he or she will never be the same! Is the most fulfilling part of ministry I experience!

What Paul describes as the love of God reminds me how God showed the prophet Ezekiel the river flowing out of the temple (see Ezek. 47:2-5). Ezekiel began to enter into the river, first it was ankle deep. Then he saw that the water was brought up to his knee. Ezekiel journeyed farther and farther into the river until he found a deep, mighty rushing river that he could not even swim across. God wants to bring us deeper into the river corporately as well as individually. When we have encountered His love, we can impart that same love!

It's His desire to bring the church to that place where deep calls unto deep (see Ps. 42:7). The glory of God is like a river; there are deeper and deeper levels. Our hunger brings us deeper into His presence!

It is so important that we remind ourselves of when we first encountered the love of God. It is vital that we return to that foundation, reminding ourselves of when we were first touched by God's love and presence.

I believe there is an anointing for compassion. Healing and miracles are birthed from compassion! I believe we can cultivate compassion in our hearts for the lost, the multitudes, and for those in need of healing!

> *Now hope does not disappoint,* ***because the love of God has been poured out in our hearts*** *by the Holy Spirit who was given to us* (Romans 5:5).

The love of God has been fully manifested in our hearts, so we can impart to others the experience of His love, and so that others can step into that same encounter with the love of God! I once heard Pastor Bill Johnson say, "Biblical compassion always has the heart of God in mind. It lives from an awareness of His heartbeat for people."[1]

After Jesus' resurrection, Jesus appeared to His disciples in His glorified form and commanded them to wait until they received the infilling of the Holy Spirit. He said:

> *You shall receive* ***power*** *when the Holy Spirit has come upon you; and you shall be witnesses to Me in Jerusalem, and in all Judea and Samaria, and to the end of the earth* (Acts 1:8).

We know that word "power" translates in the Greek to *dunamis*, dynamite explosive power! I want you to also look at the word "witnesses" in this verse. It means to be a *proof provider!* The very reason that you and

I have been filled with *dunamis* power is so we can supply the proof to a lost and dying world that Christ has risen! We are called to demonstrate to the world the power of the gospel, the power of His resurrection!

The world is looking to see if Jesus was truly raised from the dead, and you and I are called to minister that truth as proof providers! The world is looking for something real, something that cannot be fabricated. Through miracles, signs, and wonders, we supply the proof of Christ's resurrection. Only the power of the Holy Spirit enables the church to reach the multitudes. Jesus is a full and complete expression of that in His earthly ministry.

> *When He had come down from the mountain, great multitudes followed Him. And behold, a leper came and worshiped Him, saying, "Lord, if You are willing, You can make me clean." Then Jesus put out His hand and touched him, saying, "I am willing; be cleansed." Immediately his leprosy was cleansed. (Matthew 8:1-3).*

The miracle of Jesus cleansing the leper reveals the key to Jesus' earthly ministry. Ministry is all about loving God and loving people. Jesus ministered upon the mountain all night and then ministered to the leper. He is our greatest model of a ministry gift.

The motivation of our heart cannot be selfish ambition. It cannot be for the miraculous alone. The motivation of our heart must to reveal the heart of the Father to the lost, to the afflicted, and to the brokenhearted. In this way, we are connected to the Father's heart and will always remain fruitful! We can never go wrong being motivated out of love!

HEALINGS IN NEW YORK

Recently my wife and I were in New York ministering together, and we had just finished a five-day conference in Rochester with my brother

Charlie. Friday night, as I ministered, there was a supernatural joy that broke out on the people and many were healed of deafness! In one of the services, my brother had ministered and a woman's colon had supernaturally grown back! It was an incredible creative miracle!

My wife and I were later scheduled to minister in a little church in Buffalo. Saturday night was a great service; many were filled with fresh fire and supernatural joy. God restored hearing to a woman who was more than 50 percent deaf in her left ear for thirty-five years! That Sunday morning, we were scheduled to minister in a small church in Olean, New York. To be honest, we were a bit tired from the previous week's services. Arriving at the service that morning, I could sense there was an expectancy, a hunger and a desperation for God's presence!

I felt an electricity go through my body as we were all worshipping. There was a strong healing glory that manifested in the service. As I began to get words of knowledge, I knew that the Lord would release healings and miracles in this service!

The first word I called out was for a woman who had a leg shorter than the other. A woman came in response to the word; she came limping down the aisle. I asked the ushers to get her a chair, and as I prayed, God supernaturally grew her leg! She got up and began to dance and testify of what God did! Got not only grew her leg out, but healed her spine and hip as well. She was in need of a hip replacement. The doctors told her that she would be in a wheelchair due to her hip and spinal condition, but God gave her a miracle, and for the first time in years she could walk with full mobility, without pain!

In the same service, by word of knowledge I called out a word for a woman with tumors. A woman came in response to the word, and the woman's eleven-year-old daughter was standing beside her weeping uncontrollably. I felt a wave of compassion hit me as I looked upon this woman and her daughter.

As I prayed, I could feel power, or virtue, being released from me. I know what Jesus meant when He said, *"Somebody touched Me, for I perceived power going out from Me"* (Luke 8:46). I felt that same power go into that woman! She had recently been diagnosed with multiple tumors in her abdomen. The doctors had the X-rays, and she was scheduled for a total hysterectomy on Wednesday. However, when she returned to the doctors on Wednesday for surgery, the doctors couldn't find the tumors, and they sent her home with a clean bill of health! I knew as I prayed for her that she was going to be healed! I have never been so certain that God was going to supply a healing for someone as He did for that woman! What God reveals, He heals!

THE WORD OF KNOWLEDGE

*But the manifestation of the Spirit is given to each one for the profit of all: for to one is given the word of wisdom through the Spirit, to another the **word of knowledge** through the same Spirit"* (1 Corinthians 12:7-8).

The word "manifestation" means *expression*. It could be said that every expression, or manifestation of the gifts of the Spirit, holds a purpose of wooing the bride closer to Himself. They are for the purpose of drawing the lost out of darkness into the marvelous light!

I want to take a moment to talk about the importance of the gift of the word of knowledge mentioned in First Corinthians 12 and how it plays a role in bringing others into the full manifestation of their healing. This is a gift that is closely linked with the gift of healing! I would say that these gifts work side by side. The word of knowledge helps to build faith in others to receive healing.

When this gift is in manifestation, it helps others to see that God knows about their current condition, and about the disease or symptom that they are experiencing. The word of knowledge is not just subject to healing, but has an important role in the area of healing and miracles in general. There is something so powerful about this gift as it imparts faith into others for them to step into their miracle!

> Supernatural revelation by the Holy Spirit about a person's life. The information is not solely discerned, but includes specific facts that will help bring someone's heart closer to the mind of God. Words of knowledge help people feel known by God so they will believe more deeply in the truth. A word of knowledge usually comes right before a prophecy, healing, or miracle in order to bring faith for its release.[2]

William Branham moved in an extremely accurate word of knowledge. When this gift was in manifestation, Branham would operate in this gift with extreme accuracy on an incredibly high level. He would receive names, addresses, birth dates, and could even describe what someone ate for breakfast! As the people in the audience would receive these words of knowledge, their faith would rise, and as Branham would begin to operate in the healing anointing, they would be completely healed!

> Branham saw events before they took place. He used to look into people's lives by the Spirit. The late Demos Shakarian told me that when he asked Brother Branham, "How do you do it? Branham said it was almost as if he pulled himself over a wall through his faith and looked into people's lives."[3]

In a vision, William Branham saw a young man die in a motorcycle accident. He saw that God would raise the boy from the dead. Branham later told many about the vision. Even whole congregations during his healing campaign. He would often tell the people to write the vision in the flyleaf of their Bible as he declared that this vision would come to pass! As Branham was in Finland with Jack Moore and Gordon Lindsay, the vision of the accident took place. The boy died instantly. As William Branham stepped out of the car to look at the boy's dead body, he suddenly realized this to be the vision!

Branham then said, "Brother Lindsay, remember that vision I told you in America, the one about the boy being raised from the dead? Open your Bibles and read to me what is written about it in the flyleaf." Jack Moore flipped open his Bible and quickly read what he had written two years before: "Brown hair...brown eyes...between eight and ten years old...poorly dressed in foreign clothes...disfigured by an accident...a land with lapped rocks and evergreens, Brother Branham, this sure meets the description."[4]

Branham saw the vision unfold right before his eyes. He knew that the Lord would raise him from the dead. As he began to pray over the boy, life came back into his body and he was raised from the dead. The crowd that had gathered was completely astonished by the miracle of the boy raised from the dead!

Kenneth Hagin described the word of knowledge like this: "The word of knowledge is a supernatural revelation by the Holy Ghost of certain facts in the mind of God."[5]

The word of knowledge works closely with the healing anointing and the miracle anointing. I had received a word of knowledge for a woman who needed healing in her neck as the result of being involved in two car accidents. I began to pray for her over a live broadcast and God healed her and brought total restoration to her neck! There was also a woman I had prayed for on the same broadcast who had multiple cysts in her neck. As I prayed for the release of the healing anointing, God dissolved the cysts! On another separate live broadcast, I had released a word of knowledge for pain in the back and neck. In response, a woman who had suffered from twenty years of constant pain was instantly healed!

One time, my wife and I were ministering in Winfield, Oklahoma, and I had given a word of knowledge for someone who needed healing in the discs of their back. A woman came in response for the word; she had spinal stenosis and was in need of two back surgeries. For over three years, she had numbness in her legs. For a year, she was unable to straighten out her leg. She testified that when I prayed, the fire of God touched her legs and spine and all the pain left her body. She also said that her knee popped three times, and she was able to straighten it out with full mobility and without pain!

In another instance, when I was in Pennsylvania ministering, I received a word of knowledge that someone was in need of a new spine. Someone who had been diagnosed with spinal stenosis came in response to the word. The person was completely healed in the meeting and received a brand-new spine!

In the same meeting, I had received one of the most unusual words of knowledge. The word was for a man in the prayer line. When I laid hands on him, the Lord said to me, "Tell him that his life is not over, but it's just beginning." I wanted to be obedient to the Lord, so I released the word. After I had released the word, I immediately started to think that I had missed it, feeling like the word was pretty strange.

As my wife and I were returning home to Nashville, I received an e-mail from the pastor. He began to thank me for my obedience. He said, "The man you spoke over in the meeting. Do you remember him? You told him that his life wasn't over, but just beginning." I responded that I remembered the man. "Well," he continued, "that man was contemplating taking his life that very night, and when you released that word over him, the spirit of suicide broke off his life and he has been set free!" I love it when the Lord uses me to see healing and restoration in people's bodies, but I especially love it when the Lord uses me in the healing anointing to mend broken hearts! The healing anointing is not limited to physical healing.

The Bible talks about the healing *balm in Gilead* for the wounded soul (see Jer. 8:22).

Jesus was anointed not only to open the eyes of the blind, but to heal the brokenhearted (see Luke 4:18). We must contend for the anointing to heal the brokenhearted, where God can reach through us to heal the brokenness in other lives!

THE WORKING OF MIRACLES

Miracles leave us in a state of amazement at what God has performed. When something extraordinary has taken place by the hand of God, we are suddenly filled with awe and wonder. For example, the miracle Jesus performed at the wedding feast of Cana, where Jesus turned the water into wine, was recorded as Jesus' first miracle. Another miracle Jesus performed was when He told Peter to go fishing; He said the first fish Peter caught would have a coin in its mouth. Jesus then told Peter to use the money to pay the taxes (see Matt. 17:23-27).

> When the working of miracles is in manifestation, there is a divine intervention in the ordinary course of nature. For example, the dividing of a stream by the sweep of a mantle is an example of the working of miracles in operation (2 Kings 2:14). After Elijah ascended to heaven in a chariot in the whirlwind, Elisha received his mantle and smote the Jordan River. Dividing the waters by a sweep of his mantle was the working of miracles because that was a supernatural intervention in the ordinary course of nature.[6]

There are many examples that we could examine throughout Scripture about the working of miracles.

> *God worked unusual miracles by the hands of Paul, so that even handkerchiefs or aprons were brought from his body to the sick, and the diseases left them and the evil spirits went out of them* (Acts 19:11-12).

Paul not only saw healings but special miracles as well! There is something to be said about the difference between an anointing for healing, which is the "gifts of healings," and creative miracles, which I believe belongs under the umbrella of the gift of the working of miracles.

In First Corinthians, the twelfth chapter, it is said that in distributing the gifts of the Spirit to the members of the church, one was given the *"gifts of healing...[and] to another the working of miracles"* (1 Cor. 12:9-10). Healing is the renewal of the body from diseased conditions. A miracle is in the creative order."[7]

I have always felt that miracles were different from healing. A *healing restores* your body to its original state. For instance, when someone has been recently diagnosed with cancer, many times they are in need of the healing anointing. The healing anointing restores your body to the way it once was. A *miracle recreates* something that was missing in the body. A great example would be the healing of leprosy. This requires more that the healing anointing. It would have to be a creative miracle in order for limbs, skin, and appendages to grow back.

> *And God has appointed these in the church: first apostles, second prophets, third teachers, after that **miracles, then gifts of healings**...* (1 Corinthians 12:28).

> *Are all apostles? Are all prophets? Are all teachers? Are all workers of miracles?"* (1 Corinthians 12:29).

There is a difference between healing and miracle. Healing is the restoration of diseased tissue, but miracle is a creative action of the Spirit of God, creating that which is deficient in a man's life.[8]

Many of the past evangelists understood the difference between a healing and a miracle. William Branham said that "He felt that a miracle was different from a healing, even though God was responsible for them both. In a healing, God influenced the laws of nature to restore a person's health. Therefore, a healing happened over time. In accordance with the natural laws of physiology and biochemistry, a miracle happened instantly, in blatant defiance to all natural laws."[9]

THE HEALING MINISTRY OF THE PROPHET

More often than not, a prophet is called to the healing anointing or the miracle anointing. I have heard it said that prophets prophesy. Yes! That is true, prophets do prophesy. Yet it is a misconception that a prophet *only* prophesies. When an individual is called to the office of the prophet, the person is called to operate in the healing anointing, or you will often see a miracle mantle on the person's life. This mantle is upon the life of the prophet in order to see an abundance of fruit in either the area of healing or miracles.

A great example is the prophet Kenneth Hagin, who operated in a healing mantle. As he was ministering in Beaumont, Texas, a woman brought her nine-year-old daughter to the healing line.

> This little girl had contracted polio as a baby. As a result her legs never developed. I laid my hands on those deformed limbs. I felt the power go into her. I felt it leave my hands and go into those little legs. I said to the congregation, "Reach out your hands towards this little girl. What if this was your child? If it were you

wouldn't just sit there. No, you'd be interested in getting her healed. You'd be participating in her healing."

After that, I said to this little girl's mother, "The healing power was ministered to those limbs in Jesus' Name," and I handed the girl back to her mother—the child's legs just as crippled and deformed as they ever were. The woman brought her little girl back home. She began to be filled with doubt. Tears streamed from her eyes as she began to question God, "Why didn't you heal my baby?" Then something on the inside of her said, "Do you believe that brother Hagin sat there on the platform and held your child in his arms and told a lie?" She said, "No, I don't believe he lied." Well that voice said, "If he didn't lie, then that power was ministered to your child last night." She dried up her tears and said with joy, "Yes, that's right! I believe the healing power of God was ministered to my child's body last night. I believe that power flowed out of brother Hagin's hands into her body to effect a healing and a cure." After the woman said that, she heard something popping. It sounded like dry sticks breaking. She looked down, and right there before my eyes, both of those legs straightened out and grew to normal size.[10]

You will find throughout revival history that many prophets ordained by God were given a healing mantle! They would see miracles of healing consistently throughout their ministries as God used them powerfully to bring influence to those around them, even before government leaders and officials such as kings and princes! God used many prophets throughout history to change the direction and culture of nations!

We can see that Elijah, Elisha, and Moses operated in the gift of the working of miracles. They had a mantle that rested upon them for miracles, signs, and wonders. They were high-ranking prophets. God used the prophet Elijah and the mantle upon him to shake a nation and bring the nation of Israel back to God!

> *Now when Jesus went into the region of Caesarea Philippi, He asked His disciples, "Who do people say that the Son of Man is?" And they answered, "Some say John the Baptist; others, Elijah; and still others, Jeremiah, or [just] one of the prophets"* (Matthew 16:13-14 AMP).

Jesus' disciples compared Jesus to the prophet Elijah because they saw a similar mantle upon Jesus as the prophet Elijah. Similar miracles, signs, and wonders came from Jesus' ministry! As we study the life and ministry of Jesus, we can see that Jesus was a prophet with a miracle and healing ministry! After Jesus was baptized by John, the Holy Spirit came upon Him (see Matt. 3:16). Then He was driven into the wilderness to be tempted by the enemy. The Bible tells us about how Jesus returned from the wilderness in the power of the Spirit (see Luke 4:14).

Then Jesus begins to publicly declare His ministry as He recites from the scroll of Isaiah:

> *The Spirit of the Lord is upon Me, because He has anointed Me to preach the gospel to the poor; He has sent Me to heal the brokenhearted, to proclaim liberty to the captives and recovery of sight to the blind, to set at liberty those who are oppressed* (Luke 4:18).

Jesus then proceeds to talk about how God has called Him as a prophet. We know that Jesus is more than a prophet. He was all of the five-fold ministry gifts rolled into one. More importantly, He is the

Son of God, the spotless Lamb of God sent to take away the sins of the world (see John 1:29).

Jesus then goes on to say something very interesting:

> *"I assure you and most solemnly say to you, no prophet is welcome in his hometown. But in truth I say to you, there were many widows in Israel in the days of Elijah, when the sky was closed up for three years and six months, when a great famine came over the land; and yet Elijah was not sent [by the Lord] to a single one of them, but only to Zarephath in the land of Sidon, to a woman that was a widow. And there were many lepers in Israel in the time of Elijah the prophet; and not one of them was cleansed [by being healed] except Naaman the Syrian"* (Luke 4:24-27 AMP).

Jesus declares Himself as a prophet sent by God. He then begins to discuss how a prophet is not welcomed or honored in His own country. Jesus explained that there were many widows in Israel in the time of Elijah, as well as many lepers in Israel during the time of Elisha. Yet Elijah was sent to only one widow, as well as Elisha sent to one leper. Jesus was saying that there was no shortage of widows or lepers during the time of these great prophets. Yet, they were only sent to a few. Jesus was saying as it was then, so it is now! You are only sent to those who recognize that you're sent!

> *He who receives and welcomes a prophet because he is a prophet will receive a prophet's reward...* (Matthew 10:41 AMP).

Jesus, although He was the Son of God, was limited in His ability to reach people when they would not receive Him as a prophet. When

Jesus went into His hometown of Nazareth, He was limited because of the unbelief of the people.

> *He could do no mighty work there, except that He laid His hands on a few sick people and healed them* (Mark 6:5).

What I find so interesting is that Jesus compares His ministry to that of the prophet Elijah's ministry and Elisha's. I believe this is because Jesus operated out of a similar mantle and saw similar demonstrations of God's power as that of the prophets Elijah and Elisha.

For example, the miracle of the feeding of the four thousand that Jesus performed (see Matt. 15:32-38), as well as the feeding of the five thousand (see Matt. 14:13-21). There were potentially more people gathered in both miracles that Jesus performed. Many believe that none of the women and children were included in the count. It could have been even many more who were fed!

The Lord releases signs and wonders for many reasons! The greatest purpose of signs and wonders is for salvation! Another reason God releases signs and wonders is to confirm a ministry as well as to confirm the prophet's word from God.

> *Men of Israel, hear these words: Jesus of Nazareth, a Man attested by God to you by miracles, wonders, and signs which God did through Him in your midst, as you yourselves also know* (Acts 2:22).

God also used signs and wonders in the prophet Moses' ministry. God told Moses that he would use him to lead the children of Israel out of the bondage of Pharaoh into the Promised Land (Exodus 3:1-10). When Moses began to argue and complain to the Lord that he was unable to do what the Lord commanded, the Lord told Moses that He would be with him, and sent him with a word from the Lord to the people of Israel.

> *Go, gather the elders (tribal leaders) of Israel together, and say to them, 'The Lord, the God of your fathers, the God of Abraham, of Isaac, and of Jacob, appeared to me, saying, "I am indeed concerned about you and what has been done to you in Egypt. So I said I will bring you up out of the suffering and oppression of Egypt to the land of the Canaanite, the Hittite, the Amorite, the Perizzite, the Hivite, and the Jebusite, to a land flowing with milk and honey"'* (Exodus 3:16-17 AMP).

> *Then Moses answered [the Lord] and said, "What if they will not believe me or take seriously what I say? For they may say, 'The Lord has not appeared to you.'" And the Lord said to him, "What is that in your hand?" And he said, "A staff"* (Exodus 4:1-2 AMP).

The staff in Moses' hand could be symbolic of the mantle that God had given him, as He used the rod, or staff, to cause miracles, signs, and wonders to happen! God sent Moses with a *rhema* word for the people of Israel, to bring them into what God had originally intended for them! God not only sent him with the *rhema* word, but also the demonstration to back it up!

The Lord used signs and wonders to confirm the word from His prophet, Moses!

THE LORD CONFIRMS THE WORD

> *And they went forth, and preached everywhere, the Lord working with them and confirming the word signs following* (Mark 16:20 KJV).

The apostles preached and declared the Word of God, and the Lord used signs and wonders to confirm the word they preached. God uses signs and wonders to seal and confirm everything that He does! The purpose of signs and wonders are for the ushering in of the harvest. They are also released to establish and confirm both the *rhema* word and the *logos* word!

> *In mighty signs and wonders, by the power of the Spirit of God, so that from Jerusalem and round about to Illyricum I have fully preached the gospel of Christ* (Romans 15:19).

Paul so boldly declared that through *signs and wonders* he *fully* preached the gospel! Let us be reminded that the gospel is a message of power! It is a message that supplies every need to the lost and the broken! If we are faithful to lift the banner of the gospel high, the Lord will always meet us with His power to perform His signs, wonders, and miracles!

> *And through the hands of the apostles many signs and wonders were done among the people* (Acts 5:12).

The apostles were commissioned to demonstrate the power of Christ's resurrection and fulfillment of God's *logos* word! Their ministries were accompanied with signs, wonders, and evidence that Jesus was risen!

If the apostles needed the supernatural, then believer, *we* need the supernatural! I am completely certain that the supernatural is absolutely necessary in order to bring in the harvest. It is going to take more than fancy preaching, something more than a nice-sounding song, more than a nice fundraiser or potluck dinner to reach a lost and dying people on the earth! There are those who are bound in drug addiction and bound in the sin in this world. It's going to take the raw power of the Holy

Spirit. We need miracles, signs, and wonders to see the harvest come in! The Lord is looking for our surrendered hearts so that He can pour His glory in and through us!

> *Here am I and the children whom the Lord has given me! We are for signs and wonders in Israel from the Lord of hosts...* (Isaiah 8:18).

It's time the church rises up to be the church! The Word of God declares the church, the *Ekklesia,* is marked for signs and wonders. We are the hands and feet of Jesus on the earth! It's time that we as the body, as the bride, release His power and demonstration worldwide!

There is truly a new breed on the earth whom God is preparing and raising up, a generation God has marked for glory, signs, and wonders!

Some of the gifts of the Spirit pair together more than others—such as the word of knowledge and the gifts of healings, which work as a fist in a glove together! It is often the same with the gift of faith and the working of miracles. You will often find that they work well together!

Something I have discovered about the gifts of the Spirit is that you can move in one manifestation of the Spirit at a time, yet also be able to move in multiple gifts. As you start in one gift, the Holy Spirit may lead you into another.

The gift of faith and miracles, though entirely separate gifts of the Spirit, often go hand in hand and were manifested together as Moses led the children of Israel across the Red Sea.[11]

The gifts seem to stand alone in distinction, yet they blend and work together in manifestation. Whether it be the word of knowledge blended with the gifts of healings or the gift of faith and the working of miracles. The gifts of the Spirit at times seem to overlap one another as we flow in them. Yet at the same time they are separate from each other and carry their own unique mark of expression. Though the gifts of the

Spirit may so vastly differentiate from one another, it's important that we truly understand that it is the same Holy Spirit working!

As we continue our study on the gifts of the Spirit, we will discover that God has commissioned some into this area of ministry. They have been given a special anointing or mantle! Some are especially anointed to minister out of what I call a miracle mantle, and others are more called to miracles. I have heard it said that the greatest gift is what is needed at that present time. I have always believed that to be true!

THE GIFT OF FAITH

I've often heard it said that there are three gifts that *say*, three gifts that *see*, and three gifts that *do*. The three gifts that do are the power gifts! I've always enjoyed studying about the gifts of the Spirit, but what I want us to focus on primarily are what we call the "power gifts." These are the gift of *faith*, the gifts of *healing*, and the *working of miracles*.

Every believer has a *measure* of faith (see Rom. 12:3) Yet, the *gift* of faith is something entirely different all together. It's a supernatural faith that comes upon someone to accomplish God's will! It's the faith that God imparts to the believer to accomplish the miraculous! It is when the believer steps into the very faith of God!

Lester Sumrall describes the gift of faith:

> It is a special faith that supernaturally achieves what is impossible through human instruments. We observe the gift of faith in operation when God, through the power of the Holy Spirit, performs supernatural exploits that cannot be humanly explained. These exploits cannot be what is done ordinarily; otherwise, they would have no relation to the supernatural gifts of the Holy Spirit.[12]

Smith Wigglesworth described how he operated in this gift. "Smith Wigglesworth said that if you will take a step of ordinary faith, when you come to the end of that faith, very often this supernatural gift of special faith will take over."[13]

Lester Sumrall walked closely with Smith Wigglesworth for many years of his life. He recalls the story of Smith Wigglesworth raising his wife from the dead:

> One day, when he came home from work, he was met at the door with news that his wife had died—that she had been dead for two hours. To that, Wigglesworth replied, "No, she's not dead." He dropped his lunch bucket and tools, walked into the bedroom, pulled her out of bed, stood her against the wall, called her by her first name, and said, "I command you to come to me now!" Then he backed off, and here she came! She lived a number of years after that.[14]

I admire the faith that Smith Wigglesworth walked in. It stirs and provokes us to believe for the greater things in God that are available to us as sons and daughter of God. Wigglesworth walked in a realm of faith that few ever have or will. He had a great militancy attached to his believing, and he stands as a great example of someone who operated out of the gift of faith!

> When he prayed for people to be healed, he would often hit or punch them at the place of their problem or illness. Yet, no one was hurt by this startling treatment. Instead, they were remarkably healed.[15]

The gift of faith is not our human faith, it is a supernatural faith that God imparts to us! I believe that our individual faith can cause us to enter into this supernatural faith just as Smith Wigglesworth described when he stepped into the realm of greater faith.

> The gift of faith is a special gift which is given super-naturally by the Spirit of God, as he wills. Those who operate in special faith, the gift of the Spirit, can believe God in such a way that God honors their word as His own, and miraculously brings to pass the desired result.[16]

Many years ago, as I was attending Jeff Jansen's ministry school, Kingdom Life Institute, I remember the day when a woman came to the school for healing. She was 90 percent blind in her right eye. The instructor of the school asked me to pray for her. My first thought before praying for her was that I didn't feel any special anointing. Yet I knew that if I could get bold in my faith, that God would perform the healing that this woman desired. I asked her to remove her glasses and I placed my hand over her eye, and by faith I commanded her eye to open. Little by little, her sight returned as I prayed, and then her sight completely returned until she was 100 percent healed! It's amazing what happens when we simply believe God and take Him at His Word!

We can always allow the Lord to stretch us in those areas of healing and miracles where we don't necessarily feel that we have an abundance of fruit. It's not God's desire for us to be limited to just flowing in the anointing! God wants us to exercise our faith for the greater things! It is so easy to plateau when we are used to operating a certain way. We can become comfortable when it comes to certain types of healing, as we see it happen over and over again. We can become comfortable with one type of flow or manifestation. God wants us to move on into those places we have never been before or believed before!

Throughout the years, my wife and I have seen the healing power of Jesus released, and many become healed and delivered! Still, we had never seen creative miracles; but then the Lord began to challenge our faith in reaching for the greater healings and miracles, to reach beyond our level of comfort into something greater than what we had previously anticipated or experienced! The Lord always challenges us to step into the greater works!

My wife and I were invited to minister at a three-day conference in a small town in Alabama. We were excited about the invitation. As we arrived at the church, the first thing I noticed were the hymnbooks on the back of the pews, and it appeared to be a somewhat traditional church. Yet, the church was packed! I knew the pastor and people were hungry for God and wanted more than dead, dry religion. My wife and I also knew there were many in the meetings who needed miracles! To be honest, during the first night of the meeting, there was nothing supernatural that happened, no words of knowledge; it felt like the driest meeting I had ever attended or ministered. We continued to press in and believe for a manifestation of God's glory.

The second night I preached, it was more of the same, pressing in and breaking ground to believe that God would move in power. My wife and I knew that God had sent us to minister to those who needed breakthrough, miracles, and deliverance.

It wasn't until the third meeting that a breakthrough came. The manifest presence of Jesus came rushing in! Amy began to receive words of knowledge. The Lord gave her a woman's name, Sharon, and her condition, pain in the lower right side of the back. The woman named Sharon came forward; and as Amy prayed for her, she fell out under the power of God. As she got up, she began to move her back and said, "I had metal rods in my back, but they are completely gone! I can't feel them anymore!" She had been completely healed of all back pain, and

God had dissolved the metal out of her body, restoring full mobility. The woman's daughter, who was in her mid-twenties, was standing next to her and wanted prayer for her ear. The girl was completely deaf in her ear since birth. As I had my hands on her ear, I felt great faith come upon me! I could feel the anointing like fire come out of my hand and flow into her ear. I began to snap my fingers next to her ear. She immediately looked at her mother and shouted, "I can hear, I can hear, I can hear!"

Suddenly, God had performed an incredible recreative miracle! Many in the meeting were in awe of the miracle, and some were in unbelief. This woman had been born deaf in her ear for nearly thirty years due to a birth defect. God had to recreate something in her ear in order for her to receive her miracle! I was just as excited as this woman was about the miracle. Sometimes all it takes is raw faith and contending for breakthrough to see Heaven begin to move! There were many who knew this woman in this small town in Alabama. The faith in the room began to rise!

An older woman came to me in the meeting and said she heard that there was a miracle conference that weekend and decided to go. She said she almost couldn't see the road as she drove to the church because she was almost completely blind in her right eye. I laid hands on her and began to pray for her eye to open, and she could see!

There were many who began to receive healing. I knew that so many of them had never seen the power of God demonstrated this way! This is what my wife and I have come to understand—God sends us to the dead places to speak life to the dry bones (see Ezek. 37). Some places may seem so lifeless; yet, it is in those places where God truly desires to release His Kingdom and power in an undeniable way.

> *He turns a wilderness into a pool of water and a dry land into springs of water* (Psalm 107:35 AMP).

The Bible talks about waters released in the desert. That is the Father's true desire, to release rivers in the dry places! To pour out on the hungry and the thirsty in every city, in every nation, to reveal His love and power! So much of the church is ready for the release of something fresh and something new! It's our responsibility to be the vessel that is overflowing with the river to release His anointing! The gift of faith can cause rivers to flow in the desert. It can cause the power of God to rush into a place where you would never think that God could move so powerfully! God is looking for men and woman who will dare to stand on His Word and believe for the impossible! They are the ones who will see the breakthrough!

Kathryn Kuhlman had such an intimate, deep relationship with the Holy Spirit. She understood how to trust Him, how to lean on Him. She found the Holy Spirit to be the greatest Teacher, and as we develop a relationship with Him, we will learn the way that He flows and operates.

Something about the way that Kuhlman taught about the Holy Spirit and the gifts of the Spirit really stirs me. The following is taken from one of her books:

> The Word of God found in Zechariah 4:6 is a very precious and vital part of my life: "Not by might, nor by power, but by my Spirit, saith the Lord of host." The portion preceding that verse tells us that the prophet saw the lampstand and the lamps of the lampstand, each lamp operating independently of the other lamps; yet they all received the oil from the main lampstand. It was the Holy Spirit that was the oil, and He was the One that was, literally, the power that kept each lamp burning. Each lamp was independent of the other, but the secret of power was found in the Oil of the Holy

Spirit! Likewise, each gift of the Spirit operates independently of the other gifts.[17]

I love how Kuhlman describes how each gift as independent from the others, but yet, it's the same Holy Spirit! We are so reliant upon the oil! The oil pours into the gifts. Without the oil of the Holy Spirit, there will be no manifestation. We are found helpless and powerless!

I believe so much of flowing in the gifts of the Spirit has to do with our relationship with the Holy Spirit. I daresay that it's almost impossible to spend an extended amount of time with the Holy Spirit and not see Him flow through you supernaturally in some form or another! Everything comes through the overflow of His presence in our lives. Kathryn Kuhlman modeled that example for us; and in some ways, that is to be her greatest legacy!

SIGNS, WONDERS, AND MIRACLES

As my wife and I have traveled and ministered together, we have seen many healings and miracles in our journey. God has never ceased to amaze us with His power in relation to healings and miracles! One miracle that we have seen God do many times over the years is the healing of deafness! As Amy and I were ministering in a small church in Stanley, Virginia, a woman came for prayer for her right ear. Her ex-husband had kicked her in the jaw with his boot and her ear canal closed. She could hardly hear anything out of that ear. After we prayed for her, she testified that God had opened her ear and could hear 100 percent! It's one of my favorite testimonies to share with others. This woman was in tears as she was overwhelmed by God's love. I was blown away as tears of joy came down her face in amazement that she was able to hear!

I recall one of the most profound healings that took place was when we were ministering in Texas. We saw an incredible healing of a man who had partial deafness for many years. He claimed that he was

70 percent deaf in his ear. He was a music producer, and an amplifier blew up close to his ear many years prior. As my wife and I prayed, the man shouted that his ear had popped open and his ear was 100 percent healed! All of his hearing returned, and he walked around in a daze clutching his ear, amazed by the power of God!

Amy and I have often seen people in our meetings touched by the healing power of Jesus and healed, primarily in the area of deafness. As we were invited to minister in Ardmore, Oklahoma, with our friends, Pastor Andy and Pastor Jamie Rudd, for a weekend conference, we saw three partially deaf ears open during the three days of meetings. One woman suffered from Meniere's disease and had hearing loss in her left ear for several years. She was completely healed of deafness as well as from the dizzy spells caused by Meniere's disease!

God has been so good and faithful to release His glory as Amy and I have been ministering on the road. One time we were in Pittsburgh ministering, and supernaturally we saw oil come out of people's hands. It was truly a sign and a wonder. In a meeting in Cleveland, Ohio, there was a woman who was diagnosed with a ruptured eardrum. She could hardly hear out of her ear. In the meeting, the Lord gave me a word of knowledge for someone with hearing trouble in the left ear. The woman came forth and was completely healed from all deafness in the ear, as God gave her a creative miracle!

Another powerful story occurred when we were ministering in Kentucky. My wife received a word of knowledge for someone who had an injury in the left ankle. A woman came in response for the word. She said that she had shattered her tibia and had experienced excruciating pain for six years! God completely healed her that night and restored all mobility! She was able for the first time in six years to jump up and down without any pain! When the glory of God comes, it comes to recreate and to release miracles, signs, and wonders!

ENDNOTES

1. Bill Johnson, *Compassion Leads to Miracles,* https://www.youtube.com/watch?v=oghYJGQz2JI; accessed June 18, 2018.

2. Shawn Bolz, Translating God (NEWTYPE, 2015).

3. Christian Harfouche, *The Miracle Ministry of the Prophet,* 84.

4. Jorgensen, *Supernatural: The Life of William Branham, Book 3,* 179.

5. Kenneth E. Hagin, *The Holy Spirit and His Gifts.*

6. Ibid.

7. Liardon, *John G. Lake on Healing,* 64.

8. Ibid., 43.

9. Jorgensen, *The Life of William Branham Book 3,* 76.

10. Hagin, *The Holy Spirit and His Gifts.*

11. Kathryn Kuhlman, *Gifts of the Holy Spirit* (1981).

12. Sumrall, *The Gifts and the Ministries of the Holy Spirit.*

13. Smith Wigglesworth, Ever Increasing Faith; http://www.biblesnet.com/Smith%20Wigglesworth%20Ever%20increasing%20Faith.pdf; accessed June 17, 2018.

14. Lester Sumrall, *The Gifts and Ministries of the Holy Spirit.*

15. Liardon, *Diary of God's Generals;* Smith Wigglesworth on the Anointing.

16. Hagin, *The Holy Spirit and His Gifts.*

17. Kuhlman, *Gifts of the Holy Spirit.*

CHAPTER 5

THE POWER IN HIS GLORY

by Jesse

There is much to be said about the glory of God. There is a generation that is longing to see God's Kingdom advance throughout the earth! This generation will carry the fragrance of Heaven wherever they go. This next generation of harvesters are after His manifest presence to draw the eyes of the nations, for the purpose of harvest. I believe with all my heart the more that we understand about the glory and what draws His presence, the more we are able to walk and function in in it!

As the Lord is raising up vessels of power, let us continually be reminded that all the glory belongs to God. Every miracle, every healing, every sign and wonder belong to Him!

THE CORPORATE ANOINTING

There is something greater than a gift or a mantle that rests upon a man or a woman and that is the corporate anointing. In his book, *Understanding the Anointing,* Kenneth Hagin writes:

> I can be anointed myself and lay hands on people, and a certain percentage of them will get healed. But the corporate anointing has a greater effect. ...The greatest anointing of all is the corporate anointing.

When the corporate anointing comes, the gifts of the Spirit that are upon us are suddenly heightened! Whether it be the gifts of healings (see 1 Cor. 12:28) or the gift of working of miracles (see 1 Cor. 12:10), the gifts suddenly seem as if they were heightened drastically, becoming more powerful than they are normally. There is something about unity that brings His presence!

> *It came to pass, when the trumpeters and singers were as one, to make one sound to be heard in praising and thanking the Lord, and when they lifted up their voice with the trumpets and cymbals and instruments of music, and praised the Lord, saying: "For He is good, for His mercy endures forever," that the house, the house of the Lord, was filled with a cloud, so that the priests could not continue ministering because of the cloud; for the glory of the Lord filled the house of God* (2 Chronicles 5:13-14).

Solomon had dedicated this beautiful building to the Lord, made of the finest things of the earth for the ushering in of the Lord's glory. First came the praise and worship, and then came His glory! As they focused their attention on the Lord and came into unity, it caused a release of

His presence! When the glory came, the priests could not stand under the power of it, to perform their priestly duties. When His manifest presence comes, it messes up our protocol, and our agendas. Yet, His presence will not come unless we make room for the King to come!

There is something so powerful about praising and worshipping the Lord individually as well as corporately that brings His presence! When we come together to worship the Lord in a corporate setting, God's presence and power is released!

I love how Ruth Ward Heflin wrote in her book, *Glory*, "The ministry of worship brings the glory."

There are those who carry God's glory; these men and women understand the depths of God's glory and are able to bring others into it!

> The truth is that the glory of God is the person and presence of God— the glory is the Holy Spirit. When you experience His presence- the overwhelming realization that God almighty is so near you can almost reach out and touch Him—then you have experienced the glory of God. you feel the warmth of His love, the comfort of His peace. This is an anointing, in a sense, of course, an anointing that brings the presence.[1]

I truly believe there is an anointing that brings His presence. Some have the ability to usher others into His presence. Maria Woodworth Etter had that gift and ability. She writes in her book *Signs and Wonders:* "The glory of God came upon me like a cloud." She was a carrier of the presence of God!

There are some who have been so touched by the glory, that they can bring others under the canopy of God's glory and see them touched, changed, and healed! What we have encountered in the secret place becomes what we carry and are able to release upon others!

BAPTISM OF THE CLOUD

*For I do not want you to be unaware, believers, that our fathers were all **under the cloud** [in which God's presence went before them] and they all passed [miraculously and safely] through the [Red] Sea; and all [of them] were **baptized** into Moses [into his safekeeping as their leader] **in the cloud and in the sea*** (1 Corinthians 10:1-2 AMP).

The children of Israel were all under the cloud! They were under that canopy of glory. The Bible says that they were baptized *"in the cloud and in the sea."* I believe that just as there is a baptism of the Holy Spirit that we enter into and experience, there is also a baptism of the cloud that we experience.

I once had an encounter in my prayer room. During this period of time, I was on an extended fast. I was pressing into His presence day after day, praying several hours each day. It seemed like every day the Lord's presence was building stronger and stronger. I felt as if electricity was going through my body. The Holy Spirit was teaching me how to worship. As I would worship the Lord, I would feel His presence come upon me in waves. I began to feel drops of rain upon my head and my shoulders. The more I worshipped Him, the more His presence filled me. I began to sit for hours and let His glory saturate me.

One day as I was worshipping, I sat down in my chair, feeling His glory so strongly. I said, "God, I want all that You have." Suddenly, I saw a white cloud from Heaven come into my room and it flowed over my body. It was so strong and intense. I have never felt the fear of the Lord in such a way! I told the Lord in a holy fear, "I can't handle anymore, Lord, please make it stop."

Some encounters we have with the Lord are so wonderful, so precious. Kathryn Kuhlman said, "I have had spiritual experiences that are so sacred to me that I have never spoken of them to any human being."[2] To Kuhlman, the encounters she experienced in God are like precious pearls, and sometimes, as the Bible says, those pearls can be trampled on the ground (see Matt. 7:6). She felt no need to share them with anyone.

Can you imagine the encounters with the Lord she must have had? There are experiences in God that you want to hold on to like precious treasures in your heart! Kenneth Hagin recalled an encounter that he had when he was just a boy when he was caught up in the cloud of glory. He said the experience was so sacred to him that he didn't talk about it for twenty-five years. He said, "Sometimes things are so sacred friends, you're not free to bring them down into the natural."

Hagin mentioned that some things in God are very sacred. They are very special and dear and we must be careful with what God has entrusted us with. He had a number of encounters with the Lord and the cloud of glory! In his book, *I Believe in Visions,* Hagin wrote, "On this night in 1952 in the parsonage kitchen, my physical senses were suspended. At that moment I didn't know I was kneeling in a white cloud that enveloped me."

William Branham had a very similar experience with the glory of God as the prophet Hagin did:

> About two o'clock in the morning he woke up, still feeling that obscure burden pressing down on his spirit. Refreshed from his nap, he knelt beside the bed and continued praying. The room was so dark that he didn't need to close his eyes to concentrate. After a while he noticed something white glowing faintly in one corner

of the room. At first he thought it was his mother's laundry piled up on a chair. But as he watched, it seemed to move, rising up in the air. Now it looked more like a white cloud, and it seemed to be coming toward him. In another moment he was engulfed in a luminescent mist."[3]

Maria Woodworth Etter also spoke on occasion of how the glory would come upon her in her meetings, as she would be overtaken by the glory of God! "At times while the meeting is going on, the Spirit of God will come down in an exceptional manner and envelop her like a cloud," she wrote in *Signs and Wonders*.

I believe that God releases encounters such as these to plant something within us for the body of Christ! I didn't know that what was deposited in me years ago would be released through me in later years.

Years ago, my father and I both received an invitation to go to Nepal, so we decided to go together and preach. We put together a ministry tour of preaching in churches and villages. After arriving in Kathmandu, our host took us to a little village named Chitwan. We brought our bags into the small house where our host had arranged for us to stay and as I placed my bags on the floor I saw five, hairy tarantulas on the wall. Our host got rid of them quickly, and it felt good knowing that I could sleep with both eyes closed. Yet, it was a bit uneasy knowing that at any time I might see one again.

The next night, I preached in that little village and saw so many filled with the Holy Spirit for the first time. The people were weeping, shaking, and screaming as the fire of God fell on them! It is amazing to see people encounter the Holy Spirit for the first time! It is good knowing that once they have been touched by the fire of God's love, they will never be the same.

We then ministered in another village the next day. I ministered to a woman whose eyes were completely covered in cataracts. She was nearly completely blind because of the cataracts. A milky haze covered her eyes. After I prayed, she opened her eyes and the cataracts had melted away and within moments she was completely healed!

There are moments that you experience in God that forever wreck you, and that was one of those moments for me. When you see God heal someone who is going blind and all of a sudden the person can see—it changes you. It makes you appreciate the gospel so much more! It makes you appreciate that the gospel is not just something that we preach, but it is alive, and it is power!

As we continued to preach in the churches and villages in Nepal, God continued to release His power and fire! As my father was preaching in one meeting, the fire came so strong that the young people began to hold themselves and weep and scream, they were experiencing Heaven! They had never encountered God in this way before!

Hearing the commotion, the pastor actually came running in and did not understand what was happening. We explained to him that this is what happened to the 120 who were gathered in the upper room when the fire fell upon them, as they were filled with the Spirit (see Acts 2). Many of the churches we ministered in had believed in salvation but had never experienced miracles, the baptism of the Holy Spirit, or any manifestations such as healings and miracles.

One day we traveled for several hours in a jeep to reach the top of a mountain where there was a church filled with believers who had never been filled with the Holy Spirit. Many were healed as my father and I ministered. There was a boy my father prayed for who was totally deaf in his right ear—and was healed! I prayed for a little girl who had her arm in a sling; she had broken it through a fall—she was completely healed! There was also a woman who was having back trouble; and as I prayed, several cracks came out of her back as God brought her spine to alignment. We spent the afternoon feeding the people and ministering to them!

As I was getting ready to minister in a church on a Sunday morning, the Lord spoke to me and said, "I want you to preach about My glory." We walked an hour from the village to the church. The churches would be so filled with people that they would stand outside just to hear the message and wait to be prayed for. They had such hunger and desperation. Some of them would travel six hours on foot to get to the church to receive a touch or a miracle. That Sunday morning the house was filled, people even gathered outside to hear as I preached on the glory of God! I noticed that a certain atmosphere started to fill the church. As I began to pray that people would be filled with God's glory, many began to weep and be filled with God's glory. There were several in the back of the church who were on the floor crying out. I asked my interpreter, "What are they saying?" He replied, "They are saying they are seeing Jesus!" Many were weeping as they were touched deeply by God's presence!

There's something about preaching about God's glory that brings His presence. Up until that time, I had been preaching about the baptism of fire, and many were healed and filled with the fire! Yet when I began to preach about the glory, the manifest presence of Jesus would come and the atmosphere of Heaven would fill the place! I believe that as when we preach about the fire, God's fire comes—and when we preach about the glory, God's glory comes!

I will never forget ministering on a Sunday morning in Nepal when God's glory came powerfully. A Hindu woman was walking past the church and saw others weeping and being touched by God's power.

Many received salvation for the first time, including this precious Hindu woman. I led her through the sinner's prayer personally and saw her countenance change as she received Jesus!

The conditions of staying in Nepal I must admit, were a bit rough. Yet, in a strange way, I felt such peace knowing that God had sent us there and that so many had received Jesus, so many were healed and filled with the Holy Spirit. At this time, Nepal had only been open to receiving the gospel for four years. We spoke to many pastors who were imprisoned for preaching the gospel during the time it was illegal. It was both humbling and honoring to minister to the Nepali people. Their love and hunger for Jesus is incredible!

One year, my wife and I were asked to minister in Thailand. Amy and I felt the Lord's leading, so we used all the money we had to purchase two tickets to go to Thailand. We worked closely with a ministry that works with Pakistani refugees. These are men and women who have left everything to follow Jesus. They had been through the most severe persecution imaginable. We took a day and ministered in their homes and saw powerful deliverances. Many of them were deeply touched by the Holy Spirit!

Saturday afternoon, we ministered in the refugee church. The glory of God came so strongly as people were being touched by God and falling without us laying hands on them. Many were healed of stomach conditions, and one man had pain in his ear and was taking pain medication because of his condition. God restored his hearing and freed him from the pain medication! Even Muslims attended the meeting and saw the power of God for the first time; later they came to give their lives to Jesus! The Lord has placed a great love in our hearts for Asia!

GROWING FROM GLORY TO GLORY

God has let me see healings in every way that human eyes can see them. I have seen them come like the flash of lightning. I have seen the Spirit of God flash around the room, just like the lightning. God was there in lightning form, and the devils were cast out and the sick healed. I have seen God come tenderly when nobody knew He was there, and people were healed. I have seen people healed in the audiences when cancers would melt away and varicose veins were healed. Nobody prayed for them. They put themselves in the hands of God. That is all.[4]

I've always believed that no matter how many miracles and break-throughs we have seen, there will always be greater levels that we can press into. As we follow in the footsteps of those who ran before us, we can expect our hunger to drive us to the depths of His power! We will find that there are no limits to what God can perform! Through our awakened passion, we will discover, just as others have, that we can step into the greater levels of God's healing power, unfolding the mysteries of revelation in His Word and causing God's power to flow from us as a river to touch others and change lives!

Healings and miracles can happen through the laying on of hands. This is one way we can minister under the anointing. Then there is moving out of atmosphere!

> Now Peter and John went up together to the temple at the hour of prayer, the ninth hour. And a certain man lame from his mother's womb was carried, whom they laid daily at the gate of the temple which is called Beautiful, to ask alms from those who entered the temple; who, seeing Peter and John about to go into the temple, asked for alms. And fixing his eyes on him, with John, Peter said, "Look at us." So he gave them his attention,

expecting to receive something from them. Then Peter
said, "Silver and gold I do not have, but what I do have
I give you: In the name of Jesus Christ of Nazareth, rise
up and walk." And he took him by the right hand and
lifted him up, and immediately his feet and ankle bones
received strength. So he, leaping up, stood and walked
and entered the temple with them—walking, leaping,
and praising God (Acts 3:1-8).

Peter and John were heading to pray in the temple when they saw
the lame man. They saw the state that this lame man was in: a paraple-
gic, crippled from birthed, laid outside of the temple begging for money.
Peter spoke to him with boldness and authority, *"Silver and gold I do not*
have, but what I do have I give you." What Peter was saying is that he had
something greater than what the man was asking for, greater than silver
and gold, greater than anything in this world! It was Christ's power and
anointing that was ministered through Peter that brought strength into
the lame man's body, causing him to walk for the first time in his life!
Resurrection power was released through him! Just as Peter ministered
Christ, when we minister we are called to minister Christ and impart
His healing power!

Believers were increasingly added to the Lord, multi-
tudes of both men and woman, so that they brought
the sick out into the streets and laid them on sick beds
and couches, that at least the shadow of Peter passing by
might fall on some of them. Also a multitude gathered
from the surrounding cities to Jerusalem, bringing sick
people and those who were tormented by unclean spirits,
and they were all healed (Acts 5:14-16).

As we observe the ministry of Peter, we see him grow in the anointing as he journeys from one dimension of God's power to another

dimension! The Word of God promises us that we can journey from glory to glory (see 2 Cor. 3:18). In Acts chapter 3, Peter laid hands on the lame man, and he was healed! This is the first dimension of releasing healing power. Yet, there is a greater dimension. In Acts chapter 5, Peter's shadow is healing the multitude! This was a greater level; Peter stepped into another dimension of healing power, where an atmosphere of healing power began to overshadow the multitude! It was a healing cloud, or healing canopy over the people.

This is what happens when the Holy Spirit begins to move upon the multitude, and the presence of God becomes so tangible and so strong that many are healed before anyone can lay hands on them! In Greek, the word "overshadow" means to envelop in a haze of brilliancy. The light of God's glory comes to overshadow the people and healing and deliverance begin to take place! There is a cloud of power that comes to eradicate all sickness and disease! The power was not in Peter's shadow alone, it was the glory of God coming upon Peter; the multitudes came under the shadow of the Almighty! They were healed and delivered, set free by the power of God's glory!

But to you who fear My name the Sun of Righteousness shall arise with healing in His wings... (Malachi 4:2).

When God's glory comes, He comes with healing in His wings. God blankets His people with His manifest presence and power so that ministering healing is no longer limited to a one-on-one basis. Rather, the atmosphere becomes saturated, impregnated with God's presence, and anyone who places their faith in the atmosphere will be healed. All that we must do is reach into the presence for what we have need of!

In a crusade with thousands of people, it can be very challenging to lay hands on everyone for prayer. It is better to believe that the Lord can release miracles en masse. This type of manifestation of healing power is not new, it is something that many of the generals walked in and pioneered as they ministered in the healing anointing!

"Sometimes I go for what they call 'wholesale healings.' My son and daughter are here, and they can declare that they have seen one hundred people healed without the touch of a hand," writes Smith Wigglesworth in his book, *Wigglesworth on the Anointing*.

Smith Wigglesworth understood what it was like to operate in this dimension of God's healing power, as did Maria Woodworth Etter! She wrote in her book *Signs and Wonders*, "The house was full of the glory of God. It was like a mist. People fell down in their seats all over the house, overpowered with the glory of God." She would often talk about how God's glory would invade her meetings as a cloud or mist that brought healing and deliverance! Unusual signs and wonders would accompany her meetings! She carried an atmosphere of God's glory that set the captives free!

There are times in my own meetings when I can feel healing rain fall in a service, when the atmosphere becomes charged with God's power and a healing atmosphere enters the room! I have learned to recognize and be sensitive, in order to follow the direction of the Holy Spirit for the service. I've learned to discern whether to lay hands on people for healing or to get them to receive in the atmosphere! There are times when the atmosphere of God is not strongly manifested, and we know to lay hands on the sick. Yet, there are times when we sense the overwhelming presence of God in our midst, and suddenly, we become aware that anything can happen in His glory!

> *His brightness is like the sunlight; He has [bright] rays flashing from **His hand**, and there [in the sunlike splendor] is the hiding place of His power* (Habakkuk 3:4 AMP).

The hand of God is symbolic of the glory of God! The prophet Isaiah declared, *"Who has believed our report? And to whom has the arm of the Lord been revealed?"* (Isa. 53:1). The arm of the Lord reveals the power and strength of the Lord!

> *The Lord brought us out of Egypt with a mighty hand and with an* **outstretched arm** *and with great terror [suffered by the Egyptians] and with signs and with wonders; and He has brought us to this place and has given us this land, a land flowing with milk and honey"* (Deuteronomy 26:8-9 AMP).

The Israelites testified how the glory of God encamped around them, delivering them from the Egyptians and brought them out of Egypt into the land that God had promised their ancestors! As they journeyed through the wilderness, they were supernaturally delivered, provided for, and sustained by the glory of God.

HEALING CANOPY IN FARGO

As my host was driving me to minister near Fargo, North Dakota, I slipped into a vision. I saw the hand of God and the manifest glory invading the meeting! I knew that the Lord was speaking to me about the service. That night I ministered on the manifest presence of God that releases healing! There was a strong presence of the Lord that came into the meeting! Just as I was getting ready to lay hands on the people, the Lord spoke to me and said, "Jesse, I want you to minister to the people differently tonight for healing. Don't lay hands on anyone. They will be healed in My presence."

Before this meeting, I had always laid hands on people for healing. I have to admit, what the Lord said made me feel a bit uncomfortable, having never ministered this way. Yet I knew that the Lord was showing me something new and taking me to another level! I simply told the people to lay a hand on the part of their body that they needed a healing. I then commanded pain to leave bodies. To my surprise, there were several healings that took place. A woman came and testified that she had a hernia on her side for fifteen years that left her as I prayed. She said that a fire went into her side and the hernia immediately left! There is another level God wants to bring us into, and our obedience is so important if we desire God to catapult us to the next level of His anointing!

As we study the gospels and observe Jesus' healing ministry, we can see that He didn't always use the same method or formula when ministering to the sick. Sometimes He ministered by the anointing, and other times He didn't. Sometimes He laid hands on the sick, and other times He ministered through the atmosphere. Sometimes Jesus just spoke the healing word! It's important for us to know the different ways God releases healing! Then we can better understand how to release the power of God in and through us!

> *He came down with them and stood on a level place with a crowd of His disciples and a great multitude of people from all Judea and Jerusalem, and from the seacoast of Tyre and Sidon, who came to hear Him and be healed of their diseases, as well as those who were tormented with unclean spirits and they were healed. And the whole multitude sought to touch Him, for* **power went out from Him and healed them** *all* (Luke 6:17-19).

As Jesus ministered to the multitude, the Bible says that power went out of Him! Power went *out* of Jesus, because power was *in* Him! Power flowed out of Him to the multitude like a river, so much so that the multitude sought to touch Him. That same river continues to flow today, as it has generation after generation! We have the privilege to walk in what so many others did, including Jesus! There is much that we can learn as we study the healing ministry of Jesus that we can apply to our own ministries to help us better function in the call and mantle of ministering in the healing anointing! There was an atmosphere that Jesus carried, something that came from His own intimacy and ministry to the Lord!

> *Now it happened on a certain day, as He was teaching, that there were Pharisees and teachers of the law sitting by, who had come out of every town of Galilee, Judea, and Jerusalem. And the power of the Lord was present to heal them. Then, behold, men brought on a bed a man who was paralyzed, whom they sought to bring in and lay before Him. And when they could not find how they might bring him in, because of the crowd, they went up on the housetop and let him down with his bed through the tiling into the midst before Jesus* (Luke 5:17-19).

As Jesus was ministering, there was an atmosphere that came, a manifestation of God's presence! A group of men brought a paralyzed man but could not reach Jesus because of the crowd. They then proceeded to tear apart the roof to find an entrance. The man and his friends were desperate to get to Jesus!

> *...He said to the man who was paralyzed, "I say to you, arise, take up your bed, and go to your house." Immediately he rose up before them, took up what he had been lying on, and departed to his own house, glorifying God* (Luke 5:24-25).

Everywhere Jesus went, He carried Heaven! Jesus carried an atmosphere of healing power that resulted in the healing of multitudes!

All it takes is one moment in God's presence, and your life will never be the same! One encounter in His presence and you are forever changed, marked by Heaven! God is looking for people who will carry the fragrance of Heaven everywhere they go. I believe God is marking this generation to carry His fire and glory to the uttermost parts of the earth!

God is searching for those with the heart of David in this hour, those who hunger after the presence of God! There is always an invitation for healing, breakthrough, and the miraculous when God's glory is present!

THE DARK CLOUD

There are levels and dimensions of God's glory that we can journey into. Hunger brings us into the deeper things of God! The clouds that carry rain become dark, and then, suddenly, the rain falls! After Solomon had built a house for the Lord's presence, the priests carried the ark of the covenant upon their shoulders. The Bible tells us that the cloud of glory entered the house and the priest could not stand to minister (2 Chron. 5:13-14). After the manifestation of God's glory, Solomon then said, *"The Lord said He would dwell in the dark cloud"* (2 Chron. 6:1).

I believe in that moment, Solomon must have received a revelation about the glory of God! He saw the richness of God's presence, what the Bible refers to as the *dark cloud,* the thick weighty, presence of God!

> *He made darkness His secret place; His canopy around Him was dark waters and thick clouds of the skies* (Psalm 18:11).

The Bible says that *"Moses drew near the thick darkness where God was"* (Exod. 20:21). The more we press in, the more we discover the depths of who God is! There are no limits to knowing Him in divine intimacy, as He is continually revealed to us through our hunger and desperation in the secret place!

THE COMING REVIVAL HARVEST

I was asking the Lord to reveal to me what He wanted to do in the United States. The Lord gave me a dream in 2011. In the dream, the Lord began to show me stadiums in America filled with God's glory! I began to see thousands upon thousands gathered in stadiums to worship and experience the presence of God. I saw men and women on the platform ministering, surrounded by a great cloud. Those on the platform ministered out of an atmosphere for healing; no one received healing through the laying on of hands. There was an atmosphere, a canopy of glory that covered the people as the manifest presence of Jesus swept across the stadium, drawing men and women to salvation! The Bible talks about *"the goodness of God leads you to repentance"* (Rom. 2:4).

We should ask ourselves: What does it look like for God's hand to begin to invade a region, a city, or even a nation? What does it look like when God overshadows and invades a nation, when all are healed? When all come to the master for salvation? Can we dream big enough, or dare to ask for the impossible to become *possible?* Isaiah asked a question: Can a nation be born at once—saved in a day? (See Isaiah 66:8.) I believe it can! I believe the next move of God will be about the presence of Jesus, about miracles, signs and wonders in our midst, drawing men and women to salvation!

The Word of God tells us that God *"sends rain on the just and on the unjust"* (Matt. 5:45). It's God's desire to release His rain upon those who are saved and those who have yet to experience salvation!

> *So wait patiently, brothers and sisters, until the coming of the Lord. The farmer waits [expectantly] for the precious harvest from the land, being patient about it, until it receives the early and late rains* (James 5:7 AMP).

The Word of God describes the Lord as patient. The Lord is waiting for the early and late rains to come forth, because He desires a harvest! He is longing for the fruit of the earth to come forth. Rain produces fruit, and God's glory ushers in the harvest! It's God's desire to release His glory to draw in the harvest, even the prodigal sons and daughters, to the Kingdom!

> *Let us know, let us pursue the knowledge of the Lord. His going forth is established as the morning; He will come to us like the rain, like the latter and former rain to the earth* (Hosea 6:3).

The Word of God declares that God will come like the rain! The Lord comes and releases showers of healings, miracles, and signs and wonders for the purpose of bringing in the harvest!

I truly believe that in this next move of God, the church will experience the glory of God beyond what we anticipate or even think possible. It will not be compared to past moves, as this move will have a uniquely separate identity! The glory will not be in one state or location but will shake the very nation of the United States.

It will be a new move that God releases to accompany a new sound! We will see another great awakening in America, just as the first and second great awakenings! God will use many as harvesters and miracle workers, those who will release Heaven on earth, those who will be carriers of God's glory!

THE MINISTRY OF A BONDSERVANT

There is something so powerful about ministering to the Lord. The Lord so desires to be worshipped. In the Old Testament, God told the Levitical priesthood that they would have no inheritance in the land of Canaan, the land that the children of Israel possessed. The Lord told them that He was their portion (see Deut. 18:1-2). God so desired to be worshipped that He separated a tribe of priests to worship Him and minister before Him.

In the New Testament, we are called as kings and priests. This ministry is no longer limited, but available to us all! Every precious gift comes out of the overflow of God's presence in our lives. As we seek Him and minister to Him, gifts and callings become activated, as every blessing and every gift comes from the Gift-giver. Above platform, above the desire for ministry, we should seek this ministry, to minister unto the Lord! God is looking for bondservants. He's looking for those with the heart of David, those who will minister before Him and bless His name. That is the true ministry of a bondservant.

The angel of the Lord had appeared before Moses in a flame of fire out of the burning bush. Moses watched as the bush burned, but the bush was not consumed. God was calling Moses. There is always a visitation with fire before God commissions and sends us! The Bible says that God called Moses out of the midst of the bush and commissioned him!

> But Moses said to God, "Who am I that I should go to Pharaoh, and that I should bring the children of Israel out of Egypt?" So He said, "I will certainly be with you. And this shall be a sign to you that I have sent you: When you have brought the people out of Egypt, **you shall serve God** on this mountain" (Exodus 3:11-12).

The word "serve" in this verse means worshipper, but it also means bondservant. What is a bondservant? It is one who chooses to be yoked with Christ! It means the one who continually gives him or herself to fasting and prayer, the one who has come to maturity and realizes that he or she is not their own. It is an individual who has decided, no matter what the cost, to pay loyalty to the King! We are called to be bondservants, before we are anything else. It was King David who said, *"I would rather be a doorkeeper in the house of my God, than to dwell in the tents of wickedness"* (Ps. 84:10). David called himself a doorkeeper. He knew that he had a ministry, and that was to minister before the Lord.

David also wrote, *"My soul shall be satisfied as with marrow and fatness, and my mouth shall praise You with joyful lips. When I remember You on my bed, I meditate on You in the night watches"* (Ps. 63:5-6).

David loved to minister to the Lord; that was his first ministry. David was a psalmist, a poet, a prophet, a priest, and a king over Israel. Before David was all of those things, he was a friend of God; he was a doorkeeper, a bondservant of the King!

> *Therefore do not be ashamed of the testimony of our Lord, nor of me His prisoner, but share with me in the sufferings for the gospel according to the power of God* (2 Timothy 1:8).

Paul was speaking to his son in faith Timothy of the price of being a bondservant. Paul was often imprisoned for preaching the gospel. He was a prisoner, but he considered himself to be a prisoner of the Lord as well. Over and over again throughout the epistles, Paul calls himself a prisoner, a bondservant of the Lord Jesus! A bondservant is yoked with Christ as with a yoke of oxen. The Bible calls us co-laborers with Him. What do a pair of oxen do? They labor together for the harvest!

> *Take my yoke upon you and learn from Me, for I am gentle and lowly in heart, and you will find rest for your souls* (Matthew 11:29).

Before we were in Christ, we were in bondage to the enemy. The Bible says that the anointing *breaks* the yoke. We were once slaves to sin because of a sinful nature (see Eph. 2:2-3). Paul told the church of Galatia to not be entangled again with the yoke of bondage (see Gal. 5:1). Only the anointing could have made us free! Just as we were slaves to the enemy through a fallen nature, accomplishing sin and his will, we are now slaves of Christ, energized by His nature to accomplish His will!

> *For it is God which worketh in you both to will and to do of His good pleasure* (Philippians 2:13 NKJV).

Do you not see in Paul's willingness Jesus in a new form, Jesus again on earth? This is the way we are bound to go. Paul called himself the "bondservant" of Jesus Christ. (See, for example, Romans 1:1.) But we are not obliged to be this! We could abandon our faith! Could I? Yes, I could! But I cannot! Separated bondservant, you cannot go back. It costs much to come, but it cost a thousand times more to retreat.[5]

After Jesus had risen from the dead, He appeared to Peter; Peter was one who had denied Jesus three times. But Jesus asked him three times, *"Peter, do you love Me...? Feed My lambs"* (John 21:15). Then the Lord told Peter:

> *"I assure you and most solemnly say to you, when you were younger you dressed yourself and walked wherever you wished; but when you grow old, you will stretch out your hands and arms, and someone else will dress you, and carry you where you do not wish to go"* (John 21:18 AMP).

Jesus was telling Peter that he would one day give his life for the gospel. We know that Peter was later crucified upside down. There is a price attached to following Jesus. Many may want the title of apostle or prophet, but the truth is that very few want to be bondservants. We are called to be bondservants of Christ. We are love-slaves to Him and that is truly our reward!

ENDNOTES

1. Benny Hinn, *The Anointing* (Nashville, TN: Thomas Nelson).

2. Kuhlman, *Gifts of the Holy Spirit.*

3. Hagin, *Supernatural: The Life of William Branham, Book Two.*

4. Liardon, *John G. Lake on Healing.*

5. Wigglesworth, *On the Anointing.*

CHAPTER 6

THE POWER OF CHRIST'S INDWELLING

by Jesse

Sadhu Sundar Singh, an Indian Christian missionary, often taught about the revelation of Christ within us, which he called "the indwelling." He said, "Salt, when dissolved in water, may disappear, but it does not cease to exist. We can be sure of its presence by tasting the water. Likewise, the indwelling Christ, though unseen, will be made evident to others from the love which he imparts to us."[1] Sundar understood the power in the revelation that Christ lived in him. He understood what that meant, that he was one with Christ. Just as salt combined in water become one!

John G. Lake said that St. Patrick "was one of the mightiest men of God of his age." Lake recalled the story of St. Patrick: "One day he came where a father had just been bitten by a poisonous snake, with his weeping wife and children standing around. And as he stood there his heart rose in God. When presently, somebody called to attention to the snake that had bitten the man, laying on the grass nearby. And going after the thing of hell, he damned it and all its tribe forever, and they went from Ireland to this day."[2]

St. Patrick would often decree: "Christ within me, Christ above me, Christ beneath me, Christ before me, Christ at my right hand, Christ at my left hand, Christ in the eyes of everyone who sees me, Christ in the soul of everyone who knows me."[3] St. Patrick had a reputation as a dead-man raiser, a miracle worker, and was known as the apostle of Ireland. He brought Christianity to Ireland and planted several churches there.

I mentioned previously about the night I had a profound encounter with the Lord in my brother's bedroom. My spirit lifted out of my body into Heaven. I saw a man walking toward me, full of light, glory, and power. I remember the light being so bright I was blinded by it. I knew in my heart it was Jesus. I could feel love and power radiating from Him!

That encounter never left my memory; I have carried it in my heart through the years. At that time in my life, I didn't fully understand what I had experienced or the revelation that the Lord was revealing to me of the nature of Christ. I only knew that I had seen Jesus! It wasn't until many years later through seeking that the Lord began to unfold and reveal in depth the revelation of this supernatural experience.

I don't believe that we should throw around the term *encounters* loosely. The purpose of encounters is to bring forth revelation to the body of Christ; power and growth comes as a result! It could be said that with every authentic encounter, there is revelation and fruit that follows.

PAUL'S REVELATION

Most Christians are familiar with the understanding that Jesus came to the earth. He laid aside His deity as God. He went to the cross as a sacrifice, shed His blood, died, and was resurrected. Yet, what does it really mean that He was resurrected? What does it really mean that He now lives in us as believers? I believe as you delve into this revelation, God will begin to reveal Christ to you in a new way.

As the angels that encircle the throne of God, they see the face of a man, an ox, or an eagle. Revelation continues to unfold as they look and behold. Every time they look, they see a new aspect of His nature. It is the same as we behold Him in the Word of God; we are continually growing in understanding and revelation!

Saul received a revelation that transformed him into Paul! God gave him a new name and a new course! To understand Paul's revelation of the cross, we have to understand Paul's background and lineage. He claimed to be of the tribe of Benjamin and called himself a *"Hebrew of the Hebrews"* (Phil. 3:5). As a child, he studied at the feet of Gamaliel, who was a well-respected teacher of Jewish law. Paul was zealous in practicing the law, and even boasted in how he was blameless in following it (see Phil. 3:6).

> *Now Saul, still breathing threats and murder against the disciples of the Lord [and relentless in his search for believers], went to the high priest, and he asked for letters [of authority] from him to the synagogues at Damascus, so that if he found any men or women there belonging to the Way [believers, followers of Jesus the Messiah], men and women alike, he could arrest them and bring them bound [with chains] to Jerusalem. As he traveled he approached Damascus, and suddenly a light from*

heaven flashed around him [displaying the glory and
majesty of Christ]; and he fell to the ground and heard
a voice [from heaven] saying to him, "Saul, Saul, why
are you persecuting and oppressing Me?" And Saul said,
"Who are You, Lord?" And He answered, "I am Jesus
whom you are persecuting, now get up and go into the
city, and you will be told what you must do" (Acts 9:1-6
AMP).

Saul was so ambitious in pursuing after the law that he began to
persecute Christians and tried to stop the message of the cross, as he
was in fear of it flourishing. Yet, as he was on his journey to imprison
Christians, Christ met him in His glorified form. Saul received a revelation of who Christ truly was. He suddenly understood that He was
risen from the dead, that He was glorified, and that His glory and
power was housed in believers!

Paul prayed a very important prayer for the church of Ephesians. It
is important that we include ourselves in the following prayer of Paul's,
as we are the church as well!

I do not cease to give thanks for you, remembering you
in my prayers; [I always pray] that the God of our Lord
Jesus Christ, the Father of glory, may grant you a spirit
of wisdom and of revelation [that gives you a deep and
personal and intimate insight] into the true knowledge
of Him [for we know the Father through the Son]. And
[I pray] that the eyes of your heart [the very center and
core of your being] may be enlightened [flooded with
light by the Holy Spirit], so that you will know and
cherish the [a]hope [the divine guarantee, the confident
expectation] to which He has called you, the riches of His

glorious inheritance in the saints (God's people) (Ephesians 1:16-18 AMP).

Paul was praying that you and I as believers would receive the very same revelation that Paul received that day on the road to Damascus, in order that we might carry Christ's glory for a lost and dying world, to bring others into the fullness of the revelation of the cross and the power that it imparts!

Much of what I was taught about the cross in church when I was growing up was merely about repentance and the power of the blood of Jesus to redeem us from sin. There is nothing wrong at all with understanding the need of repentance and the power of the blood. I think we, as Christians, can all agree that this is a message that is needed in the church. However, I've discovered throughout the years that the church has very little teaching or understanding of the power of the resurrection, and what that means to us as believers!

The church desperately needs the full revelation of the cross. It is an empowering message and a victorious message. It is the very revelation that the apostles walked in and ministered out of. They had a revelation that the greater One lived in them! We need to understand that the apostles were not just preaching sermons, but they were walking in the very power of His resurrection!

There is something so powerful about revelation that breaks off every limitation, every barrier, every lie of the enemy that has tried to hold you back from seeing the power and light of the gospel! Suddenly the scales fall off and your spiritual eyes become enlightened! You begin to step into the power of revelation and suddenly, you begin to see yourself differently, you begin to think differently, and you begin to live as God intended—in victory and in power!

THE REVEALING OF A MYSTERY

Whereof I am made a minister, according to the dispensation of God which is given to me for you, to fulfil the word of God; even the mystery which hath been hid from ages and from generations, but now is made manifest to his saints (Colossians 1:25-26 KJV).

Paul was entrusted by God to unfold a revelation that was kept secret from ages and generations, until an appointed time. Paul understood much of the Old Testament and the prophets, all the types and shadows of Christ! When Paul encountered Christ on the road to Damascus, it wasn't just a glimpse, it wasn't just a shadow. It was the very substance of what Saul was searching out. It was the very Person, the very presence of Jesus, in His glorified form! Then his physical eyes became blind, but his spiritual eyes opened to know and understand Christ as Messiah!

Ananias was sent to pray for Saul's eyes, and scales fell from his eyes and he could then see again (see Acts 9:17-18). Saul received a new name, Paul. When you encounter Christ, you receive a new name, because God changes the course of your destiny! Paul received a new name and a new identity. Suddenly Paul saw everything in the Old Testament as a finger pointing to Christ!

A mystery is something that has been hidden. It is a secret waiting to been revealed! Paul talked about the mystery that was hidden from ages and generations, but has now been revealed. The mystery was God's plan to send Jesus to the earth, to die, and to be raised from the dead, then to be glorified, and to live inside of believers. This was Paul's revelation of what the Bible calls the mystery. It was a revealing of the Messiah, the Christ, all whom those in the Old Testament were hoping for. A greater grace, a greater glory that was promised has come! It was God's plan to redeem us through the shed blood of Jesus!

This was the mystery of what the prophets prophesied, the coming of the Messiah. The prophets of old didn't exactly know when or how this promise of the Messiah was going to come. Paul helped to unveil a mystery that was reserved for an appointed time. It couldn't be given until after the blood was shed, and it couldn't be revealed but unto a chosen generation in a particular time period. The revelation of the mystery of Christ that Paul expressed, not only reveals the glory that Christ entered into but the glorified Christ within the believer.

When the world looks upon the church, they should see a company of believers walking in the victory that Christ bought. They should see believers operating with the same type of authority and power that Jesus operated in. They should see Christians as vessels of power bringing Heaven to earth!

Within the heart of every believer lies this power, it's just waiting to be unlocked, tapped into, and discovered so that Christ's power might be shown to others! Paul wrote:

> I have been crucified with Christ; it is no longer I who live, but Christ lives in me; and the life which I now live in the flesh I live by faith in the Son of God, who loved me and gave Himself for me (Galatians 2:20).

Paul knew that the Source of power in his life was from Christ dwelling inside him! This was the revelation that Paul walked in, it was a revelation of sonship and identity. Paul knew that he was crucified with Christ, meaning that when Christ died on the cross, it meant that he died with Christ and he rose with Christ. He knew that the old Saul died, but Paul rose with a new identity! The cross provided a new identity for him; he was no longer the old Saul, but Christ had filled his life and he had changed from the inside, out!

> *Praying always with all prayer and supplication in the Spirit, being watchful to this end with all persever-ance and supplication for all the saints—and for me, that utterance may be given to me, that I may open my mouth boldly to make known the mystery of the gospel, for which I am an ambassador in chains; that in it I may speak boldly, as I ought to speak* (Ephesians 6:18-20).

Paul preached the revelation of Christ boldly and with power and demonstration! We can look at Paul's ministry and see the kinds of mir-acles that followed him everywhere he went. I believe that the power that Paul walked in had everything to do with the revelation that he received!

God entrusted Paul the apostle with a revelation that he might infuse it into the body of Christ, causing the flame of Christ's indwell-ing power to be seen upon generations to come! This revelation of Christ had transformed Paul's life, and now Paul was willing to pay any price to see others experience what he had! Paul was given a mandate to bring others into the revelation of it!

RENEWING OUR MINDS IN CHRIST

> *Do not be conformed to this world, but be transformed by the renewing of your mind, that you may prove what is that good and acceptable and perfect will of God* (Romans 12:2).

The word "transformed" in the Greek is *metamorpho*, meaning to be transformed, just as a caterpillar changes into a butterfly. As we con-tinue to renew our minds in God's Word, there is a transformation that takes place within us. We begin to grow in maturity as well as power. As we behold Him, we become more like Him. The Bible says that we are to go from glory to glory (see 2 Cor. 3:18). We should never stop growing in our kinship and identity that He has granted to us. We are to continually be transformed as we renew our minds to God's Word. The more we discover who we are in Christ, the more the miraculous begins to flow from us. There is always more that the Lord wants to reveal to us. There is always more for us to discover as we search and find out who He is in the Word.

Smith Wigglesworth said something about Paul the apostle that I find to be so inspiring: "You are to see more of a vision of the glory of God today than yesterday, and to be living in such a state of bliss that it is heavenly to live. Paul lived this ecstasy because he got into a place where the Holy Spirit could enlarge him more and more."[4]

We are all to journey from glory to glory as Paul did. Paul journeyed into a revelation and experienced the depths of God's power! Only hunger can truly drive us there!

So many of the prophets under the Old Covenant prophesied of something greater that was to come. A greater glory and greater grace!

> *Of this salvation the prophets have inquired and searched carefully, who prophesied of the grace that would come to you, searching what, or what manner of time, the Spirit of Christ who was in them was indicating when He testified beforehand the sufferings of Christ and the glories that would follow* (1 Peter 1:10-11).

We often look upon the glory of Moses or the glory of Solomon and marvel at the glory they were able to experience. Sometimes we wonder what it would be like to live in that time period and encounter what they encountered. Yet the prophets of old were looking into our day, even as Jesus said, *"Abraham rejoiced to see My day, and he saw it and was glad"* (John 8:56). These prophets were longing for a greater day and a greater glory. The prophets of old just saw glimpses of what was to come, and they embraced it as if it were for their time. They were eagerly longing and anticipating what was to come!

> *For even what was made glorious had no glory in this respect, because of the glory that excels. For if what is passing away was glorious, what remains is much more glorious* (2 Corinthians 3:10-11).

Paul made mention of the glory of Moses and how it held a great glory and was a testimony of how God brought the children of Israel out of bondage. It's difficult to imagine a power that surpasses it. As glorious as it was, there is a far greater glory that Jesus bestowed on us through His shed blood on the cross. During Jesus' earthly ministry, He declared, *"a greater than Solomon is here"* (Matt. 12:42). Jesus was saying that a greater glory is here than what Solomon experienced or what Moses experienced. Jesus was preparing them for the transition of something far greater than what was available in the present through Him and also what was about to come!

Jesus paid the price in blood for us to experience a greater glory. Why is it a greater glory? Because those under the Old Covenant could have the glory seen upon them, but yet they were never filled with the glory. Jesus did not live within them in His presence and power, because the blood was not yet shed, and the New Covenant had not yet been established. We have access to a greater glory, and God's Kingdom is within us, upon us, and potentially around us. We have the honor of walking in those greater realms of glory!

> *Assuredly, I say to you, among those born of women there has not risen one greater than John the Baptist; but*

he who is least in the kingdom of heaven is greater than he (Matthew 11:11).

What was Jesus saying? John was the greatest of Old Testament prophets because he *prophesied* about the coming of Christ and saw the fulfillment of that prophecy. Yet Jesus said of John the Baptist, *"but he who is least in the kingdom of heaven is greater than he [John]."* Why is that? You can be the least in the Kingdom and be greater than John? Jesus was making a point to say that we have something far greater than what lies in the past. We have a Kingdom within us, what the Bible calls *"Christ in you, the hope of glory"* (Col. 1:27). John never entered into it! John didn't have this *"treasure in earthen vessels"* (2 Cor. 4:7).

John also knew that his ministry was limited for a time. That is why he said, *"He must increase, but I must decrease"* (John 3:30). John was talking about how it was time now for his ministry and followers to decrease, and for Jesus' influence and ministry to increase!

Jesus came as the first of a new breed. He came with the government of God resting upon His shoulders! He came with a greater baptism than what John had. A baptism of fire! Jesus later told His disciples, *"you shall receive power when the Holy Spirit has come upon you; and you shall be witnesses to Me in Jerusalem, and in all Judea and Samaria, and to the end of the earth"* (Acts 1:8). Jesus promised them the baptism of fire!

The word "power" is translated as *dunamis*, dynamite, explosive power! After Jesus promised His disciples the infilling of the power of the Holy Spirit, the 120 gathered in the upper room waiting and believing for the full manifestation of that promise!

When the Day of Pentecost had fully come, they were all with one accord in one place. And suddenly there came a sound from heaven, as of a rushing mighty wind, and

it filled the whole house where they were sitting. Then
there appeared to them divided tongues, as of fire, and
one sat upon each of them. And they were all filled with
the Holy Spirit and began to speak with other tongues,
as the Spirit gave them utterance (Acts 2:1-4).

As they were gathered in the upper room, all of a sudden Heaven came, the fire fell. They were filled with fire as the Bible says they were *"endued with power from on high"* (Luke 24:49).

The word "endued" means to be clothed with power! Like putting on a cloak or garment of power!

In the upper room, believers became immersed in the person of the Holy Spirit! The blood of Jesus made a way for Heaven to fill 120 disciples simultaneously! They were not only clothed with power, they were filled with Heaven! The men and women in that upper room became the very house of God! The moment that we invite the Holy Spirit into our lives, we are asking the Lord for a visitation—to be filled with the very same power that the disciples received in the upper room! When we step into that experience, it is as Jesus said, *"out of his heart will flow rivers of living water"* (John 7:38).

We speak the wisdom of God in a mystery, even the
hidden wisdom, which God ordained before the ages for
our glory; which none of the rulers of this age knew; for
had they known, they would not have crucified the Lord
of glory (1 Corinthians 2:7-8).

The Bible says that Jesus went to the cross for our glory. The enemy didn't understand God's plan, he simply saw Jesus as a man anointed by God, full of faith and power, healing the sick, raising the dead, and casting out devils! Jesus was bringing Heaven to earth and transforming regions and cities. The enemy thought to himself, *If I can get rid of this one man, then everything will go back to the way it was.* What the enemy didn't know was that sending Jesus to the cross was God's plan all along. Jesus made a way through His sacrifice and His shed blood for His Kingdom and all its power to live inside of us as believers. That we might further advance God's Kingdom on earth!

In this manner, Jesus multiplied Himself and His ministry, causing us to be filled with the same power and Kingdom that He daily walked in. In this way, we might become like Jesus in that He was healing the sick, casting out devils, and raising the dead. The same power that enables others to move in the miraculous is housed within us, as we have now become the very dwelling place of God.

A NEW NATURE THROUGH CHRIST

Jesus went to the cross for the purpose of producing others like Him. We are to resemble Christ's power and character to others!

John G. Lake said, "Jesus never intended Christians to be an imitation. They were to be bone of His bone and flesh of His flesh and soul of His soul and spirit of His Spirit. And, this, He becomes to us the Son of God, Saviour and Redeemer forever, and we are made one with Him both in purpose and being."[5]

When Adam fell into sin, we were reproduced after Adam. Adam didn't know what the repercussions of his actions would be when he sinned. He caused his pure bloodline to be contaminated, so that every child born after Adam would be affected by his sin. This caused us to resemble Adam. Every child born after Adam would inherit a sinful nature. We became sinners by nature (see Eph. 2:3).

This was not what God intended to happen in the beginning. God's plan was to send His Son Jesus, the second Adam, so He would undo the mistakes made in the Garden, and bring restoration to His sons and daughters through His blood (see 1 Cor. 15:45). Jesus restored us to a place of kinship and dominion. It was God's intention for Jesus to go to the cross and bring about a new breed, those who would resemble Him in His earthly ministry, walking in power and authority just as He did! Jesus produced others like Himself, just as Adam did. Only Jesus produced a family of sons and daughters who would walk in the same power and authority that God originally intended for believers to walk in. Through Adam, we had received a fallen nature—but in Christ, we receive His nature!

> By which have been given to us exceedingly great and precious promises, that through these you may be partakers of the divine nature... (2 Peter 1:4).

Notice that Peter calls us *"partakers of the divine nature."* It is a nature that empowers us to walk as Jesus walked in the fruits of the Spirit and in the power of the Spirit! When we become born again, our DNA changes. We receive a new nature, not the sinful fallen nature that Adam received. When we accept Christ as our Savior and confess Him as Lord, everything changes (see Rom. 10:9). Is this to say that Christians do not sin or that we are to do away with a lifestyle of repentance? No, absolutely not. We have been given a responsibility as new creations in Christ to walk in the authority and dominion that we have received over the enemy and over sin!

COMMUNION AND CHRIST'S NATURE

The revelation of communion has everything to do with our identity in Christ and our participation in what Christ accomplished on the cross for us. It is something that the early church fathers held dear. As we explore the depth of the meaning of communion and its purpose, I want you be mindful that there is much more to communion than just the natural elements. The revelation of communion makes known the power that the apostles walked in. They walked in the supernatural;

that is how the church was birthed, through healings, miracles, signs, and wonders!

The very core of our identity is to be supernatural. Jesus made a way through His blood to produce others like Him, those with a nature like His who would walk in the miraculous as He did in His earthly ministry. The apostles believed that communion revealed the essence of who Christ is, His sacrifice, and the victory that He supplied.

So often when we partake of the elements of communion, we think of all that Jesus sacrificed, and we often think of the forgiveness that He granted us. I am not saying we shouldn't be thankful for these things, but we should also be mindful of the glory He stepped into after His resurrection, the victory that He has given us and the power and authority that He has granted us as believers!

To those in the early church, communion was very sacred. Why is it important to understand the meaning of the bread and the wine? Because it has everything to do with Christ's power and nature living in us as believers!

> *Then Jesus said to them, "Most assuredly, I say to you, unless you eat the flesh of the Son of Man and drink His blood, you have no life in you"* (John 6:53 KJV).

Many could not understand the strong statement that Jesus made, because Jesus was talking about Himself as the Word. Jesus is the Word. The Bible says that *"the Word was made flesh"* (John 1:14). Jesus often said things that His disciples could not fully understand. It wasn't until after the cross that the Holy Spirit brought remembrance to them of things that Jesus said. Jesus was talking about us feeding on His Word and how it releases His presence and His life into us as believers. Jesus said His words are spirit and life (see John 6:63).

The children of Israel walked in divine health because they ate the manna that the Lord caused to rain down in the wilderness. The Bible says that there was not a feeble one among them (see Ps. 105:37). This was a type of the Word of God. Jesus said, *"I am the bread of life"* (John 6:48).

> *When He had given thanks, He broke it and said, "Take, eat; this is My body which is broken for you; do this in remembrance of Me." In the same manner He also took the cup after supper, saying, "This cup is the new covenant in My blood. This do, as often as you drink it, in remembrance of Me"* (1 Corinthians 11:24-25).

Many Catholics, as well as non-Catholics, believe in transubstantiation, which means the bread and the wine presented on the altar become the body and blood of Christ. Then there are other Christians who believe that communion is simply symbolic. This is what John G. Lake said in reference to this issue:

> Jesus sat with his disciples and ate with them, both bread and fish. He went to the mount and ascended before them to glory, while their eyes beheld. What happened to the fish and the bread that He had eaten? I tell you, there is a transmutation. That which is natural becomes spiritual. That which was natural, was changed by the power of God into the life of God, into the nature of God, into the substance of God, into the glory of God.[6]

I believe that we are partaking of communion every time we feed upon the Word of God and allow revelation to fill our hearts. The very nature, life, and presence of Jesus comes within us and we behold Him in the Scriptures.

Early Christians and many of the church leaders practiced communion and understood the revelation it contains and the power it holds.

> *And He took bread, gave thanks and broke it, and gave it to them, saying, "This is My body which is given for you; do this in remembrance of Me"* (Luke 22:19).

The word "thanks" translates to *eucharisteo*. The practice of partaking of the Lord's Supper is called Eucharist by the Catholic Church or Holy Communion by most Protestants.

> The blood of our Lord, indeed is twofold. There is His corporeal Blood, by which we are anointed. That is to say, to drink the blood of Jesus is to share in His immortality. The strength of the Word is the Spirit, just as the blood is the strength of the body. Similarly, as wine is blended with water, so is the Spirit with man. The one, the watered wine, nourishes in faith, while the other, the Spirit, leads us on to immortality. The union of both, however, of the drink and of the Word, is called the Eucharist, a praiseworthy and excellent gift. Those who partake of it in faith are sanctified in body and in soul. By the will of the father, the divine mixture, man, is mystically united to the Spirit and to the Word.
>
> —St. Clement of Alexandria,
> The Instructor of the Children

> Therefore with the fullest assurance let us partake as of the Body and Blood of Christ: for in the figure of Bread is given is given to thee His Body, and in the figure of Wine His Blood; that thou by partaking of the Body and Blood of Christ, mightest be made of the same Body and the same Blood with Him. For thus we come

to bear Christ in us, because His Body and Blood are diffused through our members; thus it is that, according to the blessed Peter, (we become partakers of the divine nature). [2 Peter 1:4]

—ST. CYRIL OF JERUSALEM
Catechetical Lectures

That which was from the beginning, which we have heard, which we have seen with our eyes, which we have looked upon, and our hands have handled, concerning the Word of life—the life was manifested, and we have seen, and bear witness, and declare to you that eternal life which was with the Father and was manifested to us (1 John 1:1-2).

Communion is not only in the natural elements, wine and bread. It comes through beholding Jesus. We behold Him as we feed upon the Word; it is like bread, spiritual food. Suddenly life and strength are imparted to us. Through salvation, a change has taken place inside us. As we continue to feed on the Word of God, the more Christ's nature begins to live in us, and the more we find ourselves walking in the identity that Jesus gave us!

As we receive revelation from the Word, His nature and power are imparted to us. We behold His glory in the Word and are continually being changed from glory to glory (see 2 Cor. 3:18). The Word of God is our very life Source as believers. Even as Jesus said, *"I am the vine, you are the branches"* (John 15:5). What makes us supernatural is the DNA we have received from Him! Those in the world should look upon us as believers and see that we are not of this world, rather, we are born from above. We are walking in the power of His resurrection!

And to make all see what is the fellowship of the mystery,
which from the beginning of the ages has been hidden in
God who created all things through Jesus Christ (Ephesians 3:9 NKJV).

Paul spoke of the fellowship of the mystery; the mystery is Christ.
Paul was talking about the fellowship that Paul had with Christ!
Communion is something that goes far beyond tradition, and beyond
practicing the mere act of consuming the elements of communion. It
is something divine! It is supernatural! There is a fellowship we have
with Christ as we experience His presence from within and upon us.
Communion holds the revelation that we are one with Christ. His very
nature and presence are within us.

Then those who gladly received his word were baptized;
and that day about three thousand souls were added
to them. And they continued steadfastly in the apostles'
doctrine and fellowship, in the breaking of bread, and in
prayers (Acts 2:41-42).

Interestingly, the word "fellowship" and the word "communion"
in the Scriptures translate as the Greek word *koinonia,* which means
partnership, participation, communication, communion, fellowship.
There is a deep spiritual bond that we experience in Christ, a divine fellowship. As the apostles fellowshipped with one another, there was a
mutual faith, and in it was a spiritual bond. They were strengthened by
this fellowship, and Christ in them was imparted to one another. There
was a bond, a fellowship that they held dear. Christ in them bore witness with one another.

As they spoke of the Word of God, there was life and love and
power attached to their words as they fellowshipped with one another.
I believe as they fellowshipped, talking about the Lord, they were

ministering Christ to one another. There was strength in their fellowship. There was divine revelation that went forth as spiritual bread.

For we, though many, are one bread and one body; for
we all partake of that one bread (1 Corinthians 10:17).

We are one body and one bread: *"For we are members of His body, of His flesh and of His bones"* (Eph. 5:30). When the world looks upon the church, they should see believers who resemble Christ. They should see His glory within and upon us! They should see miracle workers who are Christlike, doing what Christ did. They should see carriers of His glory, power, and nature!

ENDNOTES

1. https://www.inspiringquotes.us/quotes/1L6E_eMN1jIuB; accessed August 29, 2018.
2. John G. Lake, *The Complete Collection of His Life Teachings* (New Kensington, PA: Whitaker House, 2005).
3. Ibid.
4. Wigglesworth, *On the Anointing.*
5. Liardon, *John G. Lake on Healing.*
6. Ibid.

CHAPTER 7

TRANSFORMED: SPIRIT, SOUL, AND BODY

by Amy

E very genuine encounter with God is an encounter with destiny. I've often found that the most profound and life-changing encounters I've had with God were the simplest moments of my life. That is, an encounter with God is designed to deposit a revelation in your spirit. Revelation is an unveiling of the nature of God—how He acts, what He thinks, what He has promised us, and who He is.

When we truly receive a revelation from God, our entire lives change. We will look at God differently, at others differently, and our spiritual life will go to another level. Suddenly we will walk in more freedom and understanding because part of the nature of God was just unlocked within us. Our destiny is only limited by the level of our revelation of truth.

As I said, the most powerful moments of encounter in my life were the simplest. One such encounter occurred one morning as I was getting ready for the day. Don't you love those encounters with God? The ones where you suddenly find yourself overwhelmed by His presence?

I was praying as I put on my makeup. The day was an average day, nothing setting it apart from every other day. I beseeched the Lord, "Give me authority over the spirit of cancer." Suddenly, an overwhelming presence surrounded me, causing me to lose my ability to stand. As I sunk to the floor, I saw a series of visions. Images of people being healed of cancer flooded my mind, and the Lord showed me a book on healing by a man named John G. Lake. Then I heard the voice of the Lord say, "It's in the DNA." I thought, *What a strange thing for God to say!*

I lay on the floor weeping for another hour, overcome by the powerful presence of the Lord. When the presence of God surrounds you, there is no more powerful reality! Everything within your spirit and body reacts to the intimacy of His presence. For about an hour afterward, I could hardly speak. My physical body was electrified. I immediately ordered the book, *John G. Lake on Healing,* a book of sermons compiled by Roberts Liardon.

In the days to come, the book arrived and sat on my shelf for weeks as I hurried about in the busyness of ministry. One night, however, as Jesse left for a trip and I opted to stay behind, I decided to crack the book open. I read the first chapter, finding myself engrossed in the eloquent expression of the late 19th century. As I progressed to the second chapter, entitled, "The Science of Divine Healing," I began to feel the unearthly sense of destiny that typically accompanies a supernatural encounter. As I continued reading, John G. Lake began to address everything that God had been speaking to me about.

As the words on the page began to pulse with life, feeding into my spirit like an electric current, I began to feel as if I were being lifted into another realm. Knowing in my spirit that I was entering into a place of encounter, I laid down the book and positioned myself accordingly. I turned on worship music softly in the background and began to pray in my prayer language.

Then prayer turned to intercession as the Spirit of God overcame me, the cloud of His glory filling my bedroom. Suddenly, I felt something being deposited in me as I prayed and cried out to God. For the next three days, I would feel light as a feather, as if my body were electrified, existing on some higher plane than this earth rests upon. In the days following the encounter, God began to reveal His purpose in the Word of God to me like never before.

Now I will to share with you the revelation that He supernaturally unlocked within me, and I'm going to pray that He unlocks it within you also.

YOUR HEAVENLY DNA

Before I begin to unpack this revelation to you, first let me paint a picture of John G. Lake's revelation.

Lake had an incredibly deep understanding of Christ living within him. Every morning he would wake up and look in the mirror and say to himself, *You are the God kind of man.*

He believed that when you are born again, you are transformed from natural to supernatural. He knew that God lived and breathed in Him and that when he was born again, God filled his entire being with life and that he was completely changed, even down to his cellular makeup.

> *Jesus answered and said to him, "Most assuredly, I say to you, unless one is born again, he cannot see the kingdom of God." Nicodemus said to Him, "How can a man be born when he is old? Can he enter a second time into*

135

*his mother's womb and be born?" Jesus answered, "Most assuredly, I say to you, unless one is born of water and the Spirit, he cannot enter the kingdom of God. That which is born of the flesh is flesh, and that which is **born of the Spirit** is spirit"* (John 3:3-6).

Here in this portion of Scripture, Jesus uses the phrase "born again." If we take a look at this phrase in the Greek, *gennethe anothen,* it actually means, to be born from above! How powerful is that? Jesus is actually telling us we must be born from an entirely different origin—a heavenly birthplace!

When you are born in some certain countries, you automatically gain citizenship in that land. So when Paul says in Philippians 3:20, *"our citizenship is in heaven,"* he means that we have been born from Heaven!

> *Now then, we are ambassadors for Christ, as though God were pleading through us: we implore you on Christ's behalf, be reconciled to God* (2 Corinthians 5:20).

Did you know that now you are a citizen of Heaven, you have become an ambassador of Christ, sent from Heaven to earth? You are a representative of the name of Jesus, here to help exercise the will of God, to extend His governance, and to establish His rule here on earth!

> *But as many as received Him, to them He gave the right to become **children of God**, to those who believe in His name: who were born, not of blood, nor of the will of the flesh, nor of the will of man, but of God* (John 1:12-13).

Not only are we ambassadors, but we are sons and daughters of the Most High God! The name of our Father is above all other names!

When God sent Jesus to earth, the Holy Spirit overshadowed Mary and she became with child, although she was a virgin. When Jesus was born, He was born of God! He had a heavenly Father, and there was no sinful nature within Him, and so He lived a life without sin.

> *By which have been given to us exceedingly great and precious promises, that through these you may be partakers of the **divine nature**, having escaped the [a]corruption that is in the world through lust* (2 Peter 1:4).

Now when Jesus commands us to be born again, or born from a heavenly origin, He means for us to take on a new nature, one that can only come from a heavenly Father! Jesus wants you to take possession of the *divine nature*, a nature that enables you to overcome the law of sin and death! God's nature actually fills you, regenerating you and making you a new creature. This new nature empowers you to live above sin, above sickness, and to live full of the life that the Holy Spirit gives!

> *Having been born again, not of corruptible seed but of **incorruptible**, through the word of God, which lives and abides forever* (1 Peter 1:23).

According to First Peter 1:23, you are no longer born of a corrupted seed, the seed that was sown from Adam, but from an incorruptible seed, a new birth that was provided for you by the blood of Jesus! Think of it this way: Jesus was the prototype who came as the sacrifice to pave the way for you and I to become sons and daughters of God! Jesus became the model for us, an example of what a son or daughter of God should be like. Jesus came to empower us, to train us, and to equip us to be an army for God. If Paul's DNA had been human, or unregenerated, the poisonous snake would have killed him! But instead, Paul simply shook the snake off into the fire (see Acts 28:5).

As sons and daughters of God, we base our lives on the truth of God's Word, and not on fact. Fact is very different from truth. Fact is tied to the earthly realm; it is subjective, based on the laws of this carnal world. But truth operates on a higher plane than space, matter, and time. Truth is eternal, linked to the very nature and Word of God! The *fact* might be that someone has a symptom, but the *truth* is that by Jesus' stripes, we were healed! (See Isaiah 53:5.) A mature son or daughter always places God's Word above their present circumstances.

John G. Lake used to have experiments performed on him by scientists; he loved to prove what was happening in the spiritual to the natural world using science. He said, "As long as the Holy Spirit is flowing into my soul and body, no germ will attach itself to me, for the Spirit of God will kill it; this is the law of the spirit of life."

After I received this revelation in my spirit, my life went to another dimension of the anointing. The next week after the encounter, we went to minister at a church in Louisiana. I recall praying for a woman who needed a dental miracle in her mouth. The next day, she came into the church in amazement—her tooth supernaturally received a gold filling! She said, "I woke up this morning and looked in the mirror...it was glowing at me!"

I remember praying for another woman. The Lord revealed to me that she needed a healing in her chest and had shortness of breath. She told me that she needed a miracle in her heart; she couldn't exercise or overexert herself due to a condition related to the flaps in her heart valves. I prayed for her, and the next day she received a total miracle! She jumped rope with her grandchildren for the first time!

Another woman received a miracle in her sciatic nerve. Her entire leg was numb, but after she received prayer, every bit of feeling returned to her leg. I knew that the miracles came as a result of the powerful revelation I had received, and it only grew stronger as I continued to minister.

If you are faithful to extend your hand to pray for the sick and minister to the needy, God will meet you and equip you to do everything He has asked you to do!

THE POWER OF THE NAME OF JESUS

Now Peter and John went up together to the temple at the hour of prayer, the ninth hour. And a certain man lame from his mother's womb was carried, whom they laid daily at the gate of the temple which is called Beautiful, to ask alms from those who entered the temple; who, seeing Peter and John about to go into the temple, asked for alms. And fixing his eyes on him, with John, Peter said, "Look at us." So he gave them his attention, expecting to receive something from them. Then Peter said, "Silver and gold I do not have, but what I do have I give you: In the name of Jesus Christ of Nazareth, rise up and walk." And he took him by the right hand and lifted him up, and immediately his feet and ankle bones received strength. So he, leaping up, stood and walked and entered the temple with them—walking, leaping, and praising God (Acts 3:1-8).

This particular miracle occurred after the 120 were baptized by the Holy Spirit in the upper room. In fact, this is the very first miracle that we have recorded after that event! What I find amazing about this passage, is that we have record of what two men accomplished just by using the name of Jesus! These men didn't have any books or teachings on healing, as we do today. Nor were they educated or particularly accomplished people. But they had the living Word of God, the baptism of the Holy Spirit, and the power and authority of the name of Jesus. His is the name above *every* name!

I recall that one time when we were in Pittsburgh, Pennsylvania, the Lord spoke to me and showed me a vision of legs growing out and becoming the same length. As I shared the word of knowledge at the church, a young man came forward whose leg was three inches shorter than the other. People crowded around me as I instructed the young man to sit with his legs straight out in front of him, demonstrating the obvious difference in the lengths of his two legs. Up until that point, I had seen God perform many healings and miracles, but never that *particular* manifestation. Couldn't be so different, right?

A tiny bit nervous, but relying on the anointing of the Lord, I took his legs in my hands and began to pray. After a moment, I opened my eyes and looked at his legs. There was no change. I once again closed my eyes and began to pray. Suddenly, a current of the electricity of the Holy Spirit hit me, and I began to simply speak the name of Jesus over the man. A few moments passed as I simply called on the name of the Lord to perform a miracle. Suddenly, I began to hear people exclaim, and I heard the pastor shouting. As I opened my eyes, to my excitement, the man's legs were totally even! God had answered my prayer. I pray that you would receive a fresh revelation of the immense power there is in the name of Jesus!

After the crucifixion, Jesus had departed, but He told His disciples to go and wait in Jerusalem. He said, *"You shall receive power when the Holy Spirit has come upon you, and you shall be My witnesses...to the end of the earth"* (Acts 1:8). He told His disciples that the Holy Spirit couldn't come to them unless He were to leave; He said that He would send the Comforter (see John 14:26 KJV). When the Holy Spirit fell in the upper room, it was a message to the entire world that Jesus had made it into Heaven and was seated at the right hand of the Father, acting as our High Priest. Jesus said, *"Whatever you ask the Father in My name He will give you"* (John 16:23).

When Peter approached the crippled man at the gate Beautiful, he boldly said in essence, "I may not have what you want, the standard of this world, but I've got what you need—the Holy Spirit!"

Peter was a changed man! There were many times prior to Jesus' crucifixion that Peter was afraid, weak, or lacking faith. He denied Jesus three times, and even once was afraid he would drown as he walked on water with Jesus! But suddenly, after he was baptized in the fire of the Holy Spirit, Peter is a new man, full of power, boldness, and supernatural faith!

> *But if the Spirit of Him who raised Jesus from the dead dwells in you, He who raised Christ from the dead will also give life to your mortal bodies through His Spirit who dwells in you* (Romans 8:11).

The same Spirit that raised Jesus from the grave lives within you, giving life to your human body! God's Spirit is at work within you, supplying you with fresh power and anointing to accomplish all that He has called you to do on this earth. We should all have that experience—the infilling of the Holy Spirit! With it comes refreshing, power, boldness, faith, and supernatural gifts! You are being *"endued with power from on high"* (Luke 24:49). When you've been given supernatural faith in His name and His power, a boldness that isn't yours will begin to spring up within you!

> *For I am determined not to know anything among you except Jesus Christ and Him crucified* (1 Corinthians 2:2).

Paul said in Philippians 1:21 and, *"For me to live is Christ."* And in Galatians 2:20 Paul said, *"It is no longer I who live, but Christ lives in me."* Paul understood that the very testimony of Jesus, the death, burial, and resurrection of Jesus, is the spirit of prophecy! It is the gospel, the very vehicle through which we are saved, set free, healed, delivered, restored, and empowered!

FAITH: THE CURRENCY OF THE KINGDOM

> You don't have any problems, all you need is faith in God!
>
> —R.W. Schambach

You may be asking yourself, how do I have faith for something that I've never seen happen in my own life? How do I have faith for a miracle?

Genesis 15:6 (KJV) tells us that Abram *"believed in the Lord; and he [God] credited it to him for righteousness."* How simple! You see, when you believe what people tell you, you will act accordingly. But when you don't truly believe them, you may secretly have a "Plan B" in case they don't keep their word. But Abram *believed* God. That is, he took it into his spirit. When you believe that God has anointed you to heal the sick, then you will pray for the sick everywhere you go!

You may be saying within yourself, *I have prayed for the sick. Nothing happened! So does that mean I don't have faith?*

I recall the story of how apostolic leaders Heidi and Rolland Baker were commissioned to shake the nation of Mozambique. She and her husband received a word from Randy Clark that "the blind will see, the deaf will hear, the crippled will walk, the dumb will speak, the dead will be raised, and the multitudes will come to Jesus." To Heidi, it must've seemed unlikely at the time, but she was ready and willing to stand on the word that God had given her.

"I would literally go out and look for every blind person I could find. Living in one of the poorest nations of the earth, they're pretty easy to find.... I must have prayed for 20 blind people, and none of them saw. But I kept praying. I kept remembering those prophetic words that the Holy Spirit poured into my heart. There was such a powerful presence of the Holy Spirit as those words were spoken over me. I just said, 'I'm not giving up. ... One day they're going to see.'"

—Heidi Baker as cited in *Defining Moments* by Bill Johnson

There is something so powerful about childlike faith! It is love that propels us to take God at His word in hopes that He will use us to set others free. When we fear what others think of us, our pride gets in the way of the moving of God's Spirit. The purpose of the anointing is always to bring freedom, and to bring others into relationship with the Father. We always want to focus on the breakthrough we will surely see when we walk by faith, not on our failures. Our faith stops when our action stops! If we pray for the sick and nothing happens, keep pressing! When we stop praying for the sick and expecting God to move, that's when our faith has suffered!

Isaiah 35:5 says that when He comes, *"Then the eyes of the blind shall be opened, and the ears of the deaf shall be unstopped."* The eyes of the blind opening and the ears of the deaf being unstopped demonstrates the love of God! My husband and I were ministering in Saratoga, New York. I preached on a Sunday morning, and we began to release words of knowledge and healing as we went down the long line of people responding for prayer. We approached the last two people who needed prayer, and I began to pray for a man for healing in his ear from deafness. As I commanded his ear to open, testing his hearing by snapping my fingers, he testified to being completely healed! Nearby, my husband was praying for a woman, the man's wife, whose eye was 80 percent blind. She laughed in sheer disbelief and awe, as her eyesight was totally restored!

When we spoke to the couple afterward, they revealed to us that they had been saved for less than a year. They had been in a biker gang, met in a bar, and were alcoholics for most of their lives. But God had set them free, and they were in awe that God cared for them so much to heal them. They had childlike faith and were experiencing that flame of their first love! If we can return to that time of our first love, our passion and faith will be rekindled, and we can receive more from God than ever before!

> *Now faith is the substance of things hoped for, the evidence of things not seen* (Hebrews 11:1).

When Abram believed God, the Bible tells us that God *"credited it to him as righteousness."* That word **credit** is often used when referring to finances. You see, there is a heavenly currency; the currency of the Kingdom is *faith!* There is an exchange that takes place in the realm of the spirit; faith is the substance that makes things happen!

> *While we do not look at the things which are seen, but at the things which are not seen. For the things which are seen are temporary, but the things which are not seen are eternal* (2 Corinthians 4:18).

You have to understand that the things that are unseen are more real than those we can see! The eternal realm is more real than the natural realm!

CHAPTER 8

DIMENSIONS OF GLORY

by Amy

FROM GLORY TO GLORY

But we all, with unveiled face, beholding as in a mirror the glory of the Lord, are being transformed into the same image from glory to glory, just as by the Spirit of the Lord (2 Corinthians 3:18).

The Word of God tells us that we are changed from glory to glory, as we are progressively transformed into the image of God. In the same manner, when *we* are individually transformed, we then alter everything around us after the pattern of the Kingdom of God! How does God transform us? *By His Spirit.* Every part of our lives should be permeated by His goodness and bathed in His presence. Every word we speak should flow from that river within us, a river of life and abundance.

Going from glory to glory, simply means growing into the different dimensions of God's glory. When we are children, our worlds are very small. We have less worries, fewer responsibilities, and our understanding is limited. But as we move from childhood to young adulthood and then on to adulthood, our world expands dramatically! We add understanding, knowledge, responsibilities, freedoms, and slowly the whole world opens up to us. This is similar to growing from glory to glory. As you experience and manifest the different dimensions of the glory of God, you realize that the Kingdom of God is vast and the possibilities are endless.

AMBASSADORS OF THE KINGDOM OF GOD

Christ has no body now but yours. No hands, no feet on earth but yours. Yours are the eyes through which he looks compassion on this world. Yours are the feet with which he walks to do good. Yours are the hands through which he blesses all the world. Yours are the hands, yours are the feet, yours are the eyes, you are his body. Christ has no body now on earth but yours.

—TERESA OF ÁVILA

As children of the living God, you and I are called to transform the earth! We are commissioned to go to the brokenhearted, the sick, the wounded, and to those in bondage to the enemy's devices in order to administrate freedom and restoration!

Now then, we are ambassadors for Christ, as though God were pleading through us: we implore you on Christ's behalf, be reconciled to God. For He made Him who knew no sin to be sin for us, that we might become the righteousness of God in Him (2 Corinthians 5:20-21).

The Bible calls us ambassadors for Christ! Merriam-Webster Dictionary defines "ambassador" as "a diplomatic agent of the highest rank accredited to a foreign government." So then, you and I are residents of the Kingdom of Heaven, endowed on this earth with authority to exercise and administrate God's will.

That may lead you to ask: What exactly is His will? Let's take a look at Scripture.

> *Then Jesus went about all the cities and villages, teaching in their synagogues, and preaching the gospel of the kingdom, and healing every sickness and every **disease** among the people* (Matthew 9:35).

When Jesus walked the earth, He proclaimed the goodness of God and the Kingdom of Heaven, demonstrating the power of God by healing the sick and delivering those who were in bondage to the enemy! That is God's will, that we would walk as Jesus walked, as sons and daughters of the living God, possessing and demonstrating great peace, power, and authority.

> *In this manner, therefore, pray: Our Father in heaven, hallowed be Your name. Your kingdom come. Your will be done on earth as it is in heaven* (Matthew 6:9-10).

Jesus prayed that the Father's will would be executed on earth, just as it is in Heaven. This means that sickness should be eradicated and sent packing, because there is no sickness in Heaven! No one is stressing over finances in Heaven, nor suffering with depression! All of these things are a work of the devil; God has given us the power to take authority over these things. As we are transformed body, soul, and spirit into the image of His glory, these things will begin to lift out of our lives!

THE FIRST DIMENSION OF GLORY: THE ABIDING GLORY

Every born-again believer has received an abiding glory. This means that the day you were born again, the Spirit of God moved into you and made your body and spirit His habitation. The glory of God dwells within you, just as it did in the ark of the covenant! Every Christian has an abiding glory like a hidden treasure within them, a river of living water ready to burst forth!

> *Do you not know that you are the temple of God and that the Spirit of God dwells within you?* (1 Corinthians 3:16)

Think of your spirit as God's throne room. That realm of the holy of holies no longer resides in a temple, an ark, or any building constructed from man's hands, but that perfect Holy Spirit lives within you, intertwining Himself with your spirit! The Bible says that we are members of His flesh and bones (see Eph. 5:30).

> *For you have been born again [that is, reborn from above—spiritually transformed, renewed, and set apart for His purpose] not of seed which is perishable but [from that which is] imperishable and immortal, that is, through the living and everlasting word of God* (1 Peter 1:23 AMP).

You and I are partakers of the divine nature! (See 2 Peter 1:4.) This means that God's very nature dwells within us. Each and every believer receives this glory that abides and resides within. Your citizenship has changed! No longer are you and I citizens of this world, tied to the carnal nature that we received when we were born—rather, we are seated with Christ in heavenly places! (See Ephesians 2:6.) You've been raised up, resurrected from the dead, and given a new name and a new identity! Everything within you is being pulled up by God, empowered for a greater work and for a greater season!

You may not even be aware of all that God has placed inside you. Every one of us who is seeking more of Him through His Word is constantly growing in the knowledge of the depths of God's power and glory.

How does God reveal to us the greatness of this abiding glory, and how do we access it? Think about a safe containing one million dollars that is hidden in your house. If you aren't aware of its presence, then it might as well not be there! Likewise, if you don't know the combination, you can't access it. But understand this: the Spirit of God within you is more precious than any earthly treasures or monetary gain!

In order to access this abiding glory, it takes *revelation*. Revelation is simply an unveiling of the nature of God and the operations of His Kingdom. If we seek Him out, God will reveal hidden and sacred things to us through His Word. Revelation can come to us in many ways. It can come to us as we are studying the *logos* word. *Logos* is the *living* and the *written* Word of God. It can come as a *rhema* word, which is an *uttered* or *spoken* word directly from the Lord.

Sometimes the Lord speaks to us through other people, which unveils part of God's Kingdom to us that we have never seen or experienced before! God even gives us dreams, visions, or encounters to deposit revelation of His Spirit within us. Revelation unlocks the power of God, and faith is the medium that releases it to the world! Those two things go hand in hand.

THE SECOND DIMENSION OF GLORY: A PERSONAL ATMOSPHERE OF GOD'S PRESENCE

When believers begin to commune spirit-to-Spirit with the abiding glory within, an atmosphere of the presence of God begins to surround them like a cloud. In turn, that cloud begins to touch others!

As ambassadors of the Kingdom of Heaven, we are impotent if we walk around with the power of God within us, without manifestation! You are called to be a sign and a wonder to a lost generation.

David wrote, *"My cup runs over"* (Ps. 23:5). Your cup isn't just meant to be *filled* with God, but to *overflow!* Let that glory overflow in your life! Let it touch others and set them free! Men and women should sense something different about you. Everything in your life should overflow: your joy, your finances, the anointing, everything!

King David was raised up as a symbol of the Kingdom. He represents an eternal priesthood, the government of God. He points to the pattern of the Kingdom and the lineage of covenant. David didn't necessarily fit the description of a king in the world's eyes, but God saw his devotion to worship and prayer. God has removed the priesthood of Saul, the arm of the flesh. God brought an end to a day of operating out of the flesh and made a way for us to walk in the Davidic, priestly anointing!

> *And have made us kings and priests to our God; and we shall reign on the earth* (Revelation 5:10).

The Bible calls us kings and priests! In the Old Covenant, the king would bring forth the offering, but only the priest could deliver it to the Lord. Now, we are both kings *and* priests, because we are in a New Covenant with better promises!

But you are a chosen generation, a royal priesthood, a holy nation, His own special people, that you may proclaim the praises of Him who called you out of darkness into His marvelous light (1 Peter 2:9).

Our calling as a royal priesthood is to minister to the Lord. Jesus often withdrew to pray, sometimes to the top of a mountain, sometimes all night long! There are many Greek words for prayer that are used in the New Testament, and each describes a different function of prayer. However, all of these words translate as "prayer" in our English Bibles! One such word is *proseuche,* which translates as "worship."

Sometimes we overcomplicate our prayer. Yes, there is a place for thanksgiving, for intercession, and for supplication. But we must not forget to simply bow down before Him and worship! There is so much purity in simply basking in His presence, allowing Him to wash over you, and telling Him how good He is! A priest's first calling is to minister to the Lord!

Now when they saw the boldness of Peter and John, and perceived that they were uneducated and untrained men, they marveled. And they realized that they had been with Jesus (Acts 4:13).

When you have spent time with Jesus, you carry the aroma of Heaven. In this Scripture from Acts 4, the Jewish leaders recognized that Peter and John had been with Jesus. Was it their background that caused them to know this? Was it their education, formal training, or credentials? No! Peter and John had a boldness and an aroma of royalty that emanated from them. It was not an earthly boldness or arrogance, it was a supernatural boldness straight from the throne room. It was a boldness born out of the baptism of the Holy Spirit!

> Do you not love to listen to a brother who abides in fellowship with the Lord Jesus? Even a few minutes with such a man is refreshing, for, like his Master, his paths drop fatness.
>
> —CHARLES SPURGEON[1]

When you have spent time with the Creator, there is a sweet perfume that distills from you in all directions! The anointing can be sensed on you, and the Spirit of God overtakes the room. This is how the lost are won! They can sense the refreshing dew of the Holy Spirit upon you, which draws their spirits; a fire begins to kindle in their hearts.

When you spend time with the Lord, a cloud of presence forms around you. It is an encircling atmosphere of glory that your prayer and worship cultivate. His presence is thick and tangible; it is sweet, but yet, it is charged with life and power! God's presence is saturated with newness and change! It is impossible not to be refreshed in the atmosphere of God's glory.

> It is foolish to think that we will enter heaven without entering into ourselves.
>
> —TERESA OF AVILA

When God's Spirit dwells within you, and the realm of glory is accessible through prayer and worship, you come into the understanding that God's Spirit is communing with your spirit. You can carry the atmosphere of Heaven around you like a canopy to transform your surroundings, because Heaven is within you!

Kathryn Kuhlman is a perfect example to us of a believer whose lifestyle of prayer led to thousands of people being healed, saved, and set free. When she ministered, the cloud of glory and presence that surrounded her was tangible. When she began to sing, although she was not a talented worship leader or musician, the atmosphere would become charged with the glory of God. Then people would be healed of crippling arthritis or jump out of wheelchairs! Many people were touched and impacted by the presence surrounding her ministry. This came directly as a result of her life of prayer and ministering to the Lord.

When you tarry with God in prayer and worship, you are positioning yourself for encounters! When you worship the Lord, your spirit is delving deeper into the realm of the supernatural where you are sensitive to the Lord's voice and the realm of spiritual activity. Did you know that there is constant activity in the realm of the spirit? Angels are always moving and working on our behalf! When we commune with the Holy Spirit, we become more sensitive to this realm, and God can reveal sacred things to us.

One day, I recall that I was praying and tarrying with the Lord. As I soaked in His presence, time began to slip away from me, and as three hours soon became four, a cloud of His tangible presence overcame me. It was a smoky haze that began to wrap itself around me. I felt as if I were removed completely from the room where I sat in my chair, caught up in the thick mist of God's glory. This overwhelming sense of the presence of God stayed with me throughout the day.

As I lay in bed that night, almost wrapped in the tendrils of sleep, suddenly I felt the presence of God enter the room. The tangible presence carried the magnificent, electric atmosphere of God's glory. The air was charged with excitement and anticipation. I felt my heart beating rapidly in my chest as my natural body reacted to the supernatural presence that had filled the small room. For about an hour I lay there, not noticing the time or expecting any interaction. I simply enjoyed the spectacular presence that seemed to be ministering to my spirit, soul, and body as I drifted to sleep.

Once asleep, I entered immediately into a dream. I walked along with a tour group on a sunny sidewalk. Palm trees lined the sidewalk as we passed a little house. A man from the tour group turned to me, pointing at the house.

"You should go in there," he said. "You're a lot like her."

"A lot like who?" I asked. But the man just continued to walk away, as if he hadn't heard me. So, following his advice, I walked into the house, finding it lavishly adored with flowers. Pictures of Aimee Semple McPherson, a famous preacher and healing evangelist from the 1920s, lined the walls. In the center of the home stood a massive pulpit carved of wood. I began to walk toward the pulpit, feeling drawn to it, and as I did so, I could hear Sister Aimee's voice, preaching, echoing off the walls! I then awoke from the dream.

Upon waking, I realized I had been shown the museum of Aimee Semple McPherson that contained the very wooden pulpit that she preached from, although I had never seen it or been there in the natural! God gives us dreams, visions, and encounters to encourage us, to awaken vision within us, to take us to a new level in the anointing. I have had encounters that have taken me to new levels of gifting, revelation, and healing. Encounters always bear fruit and lift us into higher levels of manifestation and calling!

THE RIVER OF GLORY

He who believes in Me, as the Scripture has said, out of his heart will flow rivers of living water (John 7:38).

Ezekiel chapter 47 describes a river. In this vision, Ezekiel encounters a river flowing from each gate of the temple. The farther the river flows from the temple, the deeper it gets; at first ankle deep, then knee deep, waist deep, chest deep, and eventually too deep to walk through.

The river in this passage is a prophetic picture of the glory of God flowing out of believers! The temple represents the believer, and the sanctuary, the human spirit, inhabited by God's perfect Holy Spirit.

> *By the river on its bank, on one side and on the other, will grow all kinds of trees for food. Their leaves will not wither and their fruit will not fail. They shall bear every month because their water flows from the sanctuary, and their fruit will be for food and their leaves for healing* (Ezekiel 47:12 AMP).

The glory of God flowing out of you causes you to bear fruit in every season! This fruit will serve for the healing of the world! Do you notice that the farther the river goes from the temple, the deeper it gets? (See Ezekiel 47:1-6.) That is, the more that we pour out of the anointing, the thicker and more powerful the anointing becomes! The more of the glory that you spill out, the more fluidly it will flow, touching, liberating, and healing more than ever before!

> *...everything will live wherever the river goes* (Ezekiel 47:9).

The river of God brings life! That is why Jesus said rivers of living water would flow out of your innermost being (see John 7:38). When you have spent time with Jesus, the glory that you carry will bring life to those you encounter. Those who are in bondage will be able to feel the refreshing aroma of God's presence, and His power will flow through you to touch them. You are accessing that abiding anointing and allowing your spirit to commune with God's. Then God is manifesting His presence and power through you, putting you on display before the world to show His glory! This is what happened when the Jewish leaders saw Peter and John. They knew that these men had been with Jesus!

We can experience the glory every day of our lives. It is up to us whether we stand ankle deep, waist deep, or whether we will swim in the river! Will we flow with the currents of His presence, moving each day throughout the realm of the glory in perfect unity with the Spirit of God? We must desire to be completely immersed in the river!

LEVELS OF PRAYER

Prayer can often be described as a journey. Although we are taught in Scripture to pray without ceasing, there are many levels to prayer. Teresa of Avila said it this way:

> ...prayer in my opinion is nothing more than an intimate sharing between friends; it means taking time frequently to be with him who we know loves us. The important thing is not to think much, but to love much, and so do that which best stirs you to love.

Teresa of Avila was a pioneer of prayer; she would spend hours in the attitude of prayer, communing with the Holy Spirit in friendship and intimacy. Sometimes, however, it is difficult to enter into this level of prayer. Distractions and mental barricades can hinder us from experiencing this depth of worship. That is why we must follow the pathway into prayer that helps us clear away the mental hindrances and will place our spirit in an attitude of receiving from Heaven and experiencing God's glory.

> *He who speaks in a tongue edifies himself, but he who prophesies edifies the church* (1 Corinthians 14:4).

The first level of prayer would be *praying in tongues*. The word "edify" in this Scripture means to build up, or charge, almost like a battery! When you pray and spend time with Jesus, you are building up and "charging" your spirit full of life! It is vitally important as the bride of Christ to keep our lamps filled with oil, unlike the foolish virgins who were ill-prepared to receive the bridegroom! Praying in tongues can cause you to enter into the presence with ease!

When you pray in tongues, you will feel those distractions and heavy burdens begin to lift off of you, lifting you into His presence and clearing the air, so to speak! Paul wrote to the church in Corinth: *"I thank my God I speak with tongues more than you all"* (1 Cor. 14:18).

Paul always encourages believers to pray in the spirit; prayer changes things! If you begin to make a daily habit of praying in tongues, you will find that the presence of God will become more tangible than ever before!

John G. Lake was a man who practiced prayer militantly. He wouldn't even allow someone on his ministry team unless they had been heavily immersed in prayer! As mentioned previously, as a student of science as well as healing, Lake would often submit himself to scientific tests and clinics as a way of proving what was taking place in the spirit scientifically!

Once, a group of scientists strapped him to a machine that measured mental activity. Then, he began to recite poetry and prose so the scientists could measure the vibrations of the machine. But as he was reciting, he couldn't help the Spirit of God rising up within him! The scientists began to exclaim that his mental range was wider than any human they had ever seen! Lake writes:

> But I prayed in my heart, Lord God, if you will only let the Spirit of God come like the lightnings of God upon my soul for two seconds, I know something is going to happen that these men have never seen before. So, as I closed the last lines, suddenly the Spirit of God struck me in a burst of praise and tongues, and the old indicator on the instrument bounced to its limit, and I haven't

the least idea how much further it would have gone if it were a possibility. The professors said, "We have never seen anything like it." I replied, "Gentlemen, it is the Holy Ghost."[2]

The next level of prayer to enter into after you have prayed in tongues, would be *thanks and declaration*. If you want to enter into worship more easily, begin to thank God for everything He has done in your life! Giving thanks is appreciating all that God has done in your life, and declaration is thanking Him for all that He is doing, and will do in the future! I always take time to thank God for the things that He is doing in my life.

> *Rejoice always, pray without ceasing, in everything give thanks; for this is the will of God in Christ Jesus for you* (1 Thessalonians 5:16-18).

We are instructed to have a mindset of praise and thanksgiving. Praying without ceasing means having an attitude of prayer and communion with the Father!

The third level of prayer would simply be *praise!* When you praise, you are magnifying God, telling the world that He is worthy! Psalm 22:3 says that God inhabits the praises of His people. The Hebrew word for "praise" here means to be *seated* or *enthroned*. You are magnifying Him as the One seated on the throne!

Worship is the next level of prayer that praise brings you into! It is often referred to as contemplative prayer. Worship is communing with God's Spirit within you. It is a wordless communion, the deepest level of prayer.

Ruth Heflin, worldwide revivalist and prayer minister said, "Praise until the spirit of worship comes, worship until the glory comes, and then stand in the glory." The glory is the nature of God manifesting; it is the realm of Heaven, the revelatory realm, and all that exists in the throne room of God. Anything can happen in the glory!

"It is foolish to think that we will enter heaven without entering into ourselves," wrote Teresa of Avila. When you are worshipping, you are entering into the throne room! Where is that? It is within you!

> *Do you not know that you are the temple of God and that the Spirit of God dwells in you?* (1 Corinthians 3:16)

When you realize that Heaven is within you, you will understand that it isn't necessary for you to reach into the skies and pull God down in order to access His glory and enjoy His goodness. When you begin to live your life from this revelation, you will better understand the Kingdom and manifest more of God's glory in your life.

THE THIRD DIMENSION OF GLORY: CORPORATE GLORY

> *A cord of three strands is not quickly broken* (Ecclesiastes 4:12 AMP).

Imagine a group of believers who understand, by revelation, the abiding anointing within them, and are cultivating and practicing the presence of God in their own lives—and are releasing that river of glory from within them! When that group of believers comes together in a corporate worship setting, they create a realm through their worship that is attractive to the angels! This is a realm that is often called by many names: the glory realm, the corporate anointing, the realm of possibility, the realm of atmospheric miracles...the list goes on. Simply put, it is the presence of God that manifests as believers worship the King of kings!

When a corporate body of believers come together in worship, it creates an atmosphere where anything is possible. Worship ushers in the angelic, the presence of God fills the room, and gifts begin to operate on a higher plane than ever before.

God is calling upon a generation to operate in the kingly anointing, to usher His glory into the earth through *worship and praise*. The body of Christ is able to witness a more powerful realm of glory through simply coming into unity to worship together! The anointing is in the cluster, and two are better than one.

THE REALM OF CREATIVE MIRACLES

But, beloved, do not forget this one thing, that with the Lord one day is as a thousand years, and a thousand years are as one day (2 Peter 3:8).

Did you know that in the supernatural realm, there is no time? In the glory, something that would take years in the natural would only take mere moments! There is power and energy in God's presence to release creative miracles and instantaneous manifestations.

*However, the report went around concerning Him all the more; and great multitudes came together to hear, and to be healed by Him of their infirmities. So He Himself often withdrew into the wilderness and prayed. Now it happened on a certain day, as He was teaching, that there were Pharisees and teachers of the law sitting by, who had come out of every town of Galilee, Judea, and Jerusalem. And **the power of the Lord was present to heal them*** (Luke 5:15-17).

In this passage of Scripture, we find that Jesus is frequently spending time in the presence of God in prayer, and out of the overflow of which He is ministering healing. But we also find that in a particular instance, *"the power of the Lord was present to heal."*

In this same gathering, Jesus tells a man who was paralyzed to rise, pick up his mat, and sin no more. The Bible says, *"Immediately he rose up before them, took up what he had been lying on, and departed to his own house, glorifying God"* (Luke 5:25).

This was an instantaneous miracle, wrought out of the power of the Lord present in the atmosphere! Where there is miraculous oil flowing, and a people who are hungry and expectant, anything can happen!

We have had incredible miracles happen in the realm of God's presence! We have seen God perform powerful miracles firsthand, such as dental miracles, surgically implanted metal dissolving out of bodies, legs growing out, eardrums recreated, tumors dissolving, hernias disappearing, and more! God can perform these same miracles through every believer. In fact, it is His good pleasure to move through His sons and daughters to heal the sick.

SPEAKING INTO THE GLORY

Jesus answered and said to them, "Most assuredly, I say to you, the Son can do nothing of Himself, but what He sees the Father do; for whatever He does, the Son also does in like manner" (John 5:19).

There is an aspect of the prophetic called the visionary realm, or the seer realm. Vision is a mental sight, a dream, or an oracle, and when it is meditated upon in faith, it is powerful enough to mold your present circumstances. Sometimes that vision can be expansive; but sometimes, it can come as simply discernment or a word of knowledge.

Jesus said He only did what He saw the Father doing! If we, as believers, can begin to exercise our faith in the visionary realm, then we too can see what the Father is doing! Sometimes God reveals things to me that He desires to release in the services. One time I was in Kansas ministering, and I was praying for a particular man in the prayer line. Suddenly, I had a vision of the Holy Spirit as if He was a chiropractor, realigning this man's back. So I told the man, "God wants to perform a Holy Ghost realignment on your back!" The man laughed. He said, "I worked construction for years. I had a heavy object fall on my head, and it crushed my spine. I've had four corrective surgeries within six years and have had constant pain ever since. I don't go a moment without pain."

He then went on to tell me that many people had prayed for him, but that he still believed God would heal him. I knew that since God had given me the vision, that today was the day the man would get his miracle. As I released the healing word over him, he began to laugh and jump. All the pain was GONE! Two days later he came to the last meeting to tell us that he was amazed that he was completely and totally free of the pain for the first time in six years.

Miracles aren't just limited to bodies being healed and restored. Jesus had incredible miracles occur, such as the multiplication of the loaves of bread and fish. Jesse and I have seen signs and wonders manifest right out of God's goodness. Some have even received financial miracles in the glory of God. I recall in one meeting, the Lord showed me that He wanted Jesse and I to call forth financial miracles. Being obedient, we began to speak into the presence of God in the room, expecting God's creative forces to work on behalf of those in the audience. As we all prayed and believed, we began to call forth money miracles, lost inheritances to be returned, and debt cancellation.

Three days later, a woman who had been waiting for a settlement of $46,000 for six years, received the entire check in full in the mail! Many other testimonies of miraculous money miracles flowed in. That's my

God! You see, if you can catch wind in the Spirit of all that God wants to release, you can speak those things into reality too!

> *Death and life are in the power of the tongue, and those who love it will eat its fruit* (Proverbs 18:21).

All of us can tap into the visionary realm, and when you speak those things that you are seeing into the creative energy housed in the glory of God, mountains begin to move! Our words carry tremendous power. In Genesis, the first attribute given to God is "Creator."

> *In the beginning God* **created** *the heavens and the earth* (Genesis 1:1).

God is first and foremost, the Creator! As human beings created in His likeness, He has given us the same creative ability to speak and to create. That is why Paul instructs us in Philippians 4:8, *"whatever things are true, whatever things are noble, whatever things are just, whatever things are pure, whatever things are lovely, whatever things are of good report, if there is any virtue and if there is anything praiseworthy—meditate on these things."*

When we think on heavenly things, on good things, then those things will naturally flow out of us in the form of our words! Out of the overflow of the heart, the mouth speaks (see Luke 6:45). When you spend time immersed in God's presence and glory, He will reveal hidden things to you, trusting you with the ability to exercise His will through your life!

> *So Jesus answered and said to them, "Have faith in God. For assuredly, I say to you, whoever says to this mountain, 'Be removed and be cast into the sea,' and does not doubt in his heart, but believes that those things he says will be done, he will have whatever he says. Therefore*

*I say to you, whatever things you ask when you pray,
believe that you receive them, and you will have them"*
(Mark 11:22-24).

The night before Jesus said this, He had cursed an unfruitful fig tree. The next morning, His disciples were surprised to find that the fig tree had withered up and died! Jesus was demonstrating to His disciples, the power of speaking by faith! Even though nothing had changed about the fig tree outwardly, Jesus' words struck the tree at the root! Sometimes we find ourselves believing God for something, and speak by faith, but there aren't always instantaneous changes—but our words are affecting life and are impacting the very root of the problem!

THE POWER OF THE CORPORATE ANOINTING

When we enter into a time of worship as a corporate body, God's presence saturates the atmosphere in a greater way. There is a stronger, more robust wine in the cluster! (See Isaiah 65:8.) This is the realm where our spirits are refreshed, giftings are activated, mantles are released, and unity is established. Anything can happen in the realm of God's glory!

THE FOURTH DIMENSION OF GLORY: GOVERNMENTAL GLORY

*The key of the house of David I will lay on his shoulder;
so he shall open, and no one shall shut; and he shall shut,
and no one shall open* (Isaiah 22:22).

When Jesus died on the cross, He didn't just sacrifice for us so that we could one day graduate on to Heaven. Jesus died to *establish* the Kingdom of God on earth. King David was raised up as a symbol of the Kingdom. His kingship represents an eternal priesthood, the government of God, the pattern of the Kingdom, and the lineage of covenant. Saul represented the arm of the flesh. God removed a day of operating out of the carnal and replaced it with a new covenant, a better covenant!

As believers, it is our privilege to act as God's ambassadors! God has entrusted us with immense power, all for the purpose of displaying His goodness to a lost and dying world! Much of our time as Christians is spent within the four walls of the church; while church services and conferences are necessary for our spiritual growth, we must constantly remind ourselves that our privilege as believers is to extend the jurisdiction of the Kingdom of God beyond the church walls. We are called to reign as kings in this life (see Rev. 5:9-10). God's power must be demonstrated publicly. You and I are ambassadors of the Kingdom, image-bearers of God, and agents of assignment and purpose. The world needs to see God's children displaying unity and power, reigning as kings and priests!

Action is the only way to see this promise manifest. The body of Christ must rise up as an army and take action against the forces of darkness! We are the hands and feet of Christ on earth. The answer to the troubles of the nations lies within you and me! The solution to the world's suffering is contained in the life-giving spirit that was seeded in you the moment you were born again!

The mistake that much of the church has made is that we often desire to bring the lost into our world before they can be set free. But God wants us to go out into all the world, taking the love and power of Christ with us into the streets, just as Jesus did! Jesus ministered to the woman at the well as He was getting a drink of water. He told her everything about herself, and consequently she became the first female evangelist, sharing her story with an entire village! If we can demonstrate the love and power of God, the anointing will break the yoke of bondage, and the Holy Spirit will begin to execute transformation!

Go therefore and make disciples of all the nations... (Matthew 28:19).

Not only are we called to preach individual salvation, but to demonstrate societal change and transformation. We are called to make *disciples of ALL the nations!* We can demonstrate the love and power of God everywhere we go; we can transform cities and nations by simply living the lifestyle that Jesus lived!

One man or woman can do mighty exploits for the Kingdom of God; but how much power could a body of kings and priests release together? As the body of Christ comes together in the unity of the faith, stepping out in their destinies and callings as children of God, we will see an unfurling of Christ's banner over the nations of the world such as we have never seen before.

I believe God is getting ready to pour out His Spirit in an unprecedented way! Get ready, a new breed of glory carriers, armed with miracles, signs, and wonders, coming together as one prophetic voice is being equipped and released. An era of kingly authority is upon us!

"I would have lost heart, unless I had believed that I would see the goodness of the Lord in the land of the living" (Ps. 27:13). Here, on earth, is where we will see Heaven reigning. We will see the goodness of the Lord in the land of the living.

Though the enemy may take territory, he has no legal right to occupy. You and I are the enforcers of Christ's victory for our households, our cities, and for our nations!

There are many ministries today where the "church model" is changing dramatically. No longer is the local church limited to inspirational sermons, polished speaking, life groups, drama teams, and hip worship teams (not that there's anything wrong with those things!). But God is challenging His church to go beyond those things; many ministries today are training up groups to take the gospel to the streets, ministering to the needy, prophesying over the lost, and even visiting hospitals regularly to pray for the sick! It will take action on the part of the body of Christ to make it our responsibility to minister the love and compassion of Jesus with power and demonstration everywhere we go! Evangelism isn't limited to those with a platform or a microphone; every believer has a territory and a responsibility to share the gospel with those who are lost and hurting!

MANTLES OF AUTHORITY: KINGS AND PRIESTS

And have made us kings and priests to our God; and we shall reign on the earth (Revelation 5:10).

We are all called as kings, because God wants to exercise His rulership over the earth, and establish the governance of God through you and me. There are divine designs within each believer that Christ wants to release. There is a kingly authority that we have been given; earthly dominion has been restored to us!

All of us are called as kings—we each have a realm of influence in which we are to take territory for the Kingdom of God. When you walk into your workplace, you carry an atmosphere of royalty. You have kingly authority over sickness, dominion over demonic spirits and witchcraft, and you have the privilege and the mandate from Heaven to release the justice and the jurisdiction of God in your sphere of influence.

What does the Kingdom of God look like? It looks like depression being broken off of the lives of men and women, like sicknesses being healed, like families restored, like souls being saved, and like lives being changed. That is your calling as a king and a priest: to extend the peace of God into the earth!

There is no king without a territory. Now although we *all* have been called as *kings and priests*, to *some* are given a *mantle* for governmental authority.

MANTLED WITH POWER

...The effective, fervent prayer of a righteous man avails much. Elijah was a man with a nature like ours, and he prayed earnestly that it would not rain; and it did not rain on the land for three years and six months (James 5:16-17).

In First Kings 17:1, Elijah boldly declares to King Ahab, *"there shall not be dew nor rain these years, except by my word."*

Elijah had been given a mantle of authority, and he was confident in what God had entrusted him with. He was mantled with governmental authority and the ability to call forth rain, to call down fire, to command the weather, the earth, and the land. He possessed *greater authority* than the earthly kings and the priests of the foreign gods.

Many things can signify spiritual, governing authority: signs and wonders, commanding the heavens, authority of the spoken word, creative miracles, and more.

In her day, Aimee Semple McPherson was considered the "spiritual governor" of California. There was a time when Maria Woodworth Etter called her to minister at her church in Indiana; many people in that region were contracting a disease and dying. It was an epidemic. McPherson said, "When I get to the border of the town, the epidemic will be broken." Sure enough, when she arrived, the power of the sickness was broken, and the plague ceased to spread! This signifies a mantle of authority and power.

John G. Lake was another incredible healing minister who carried governmental power and authority. Spokane, Washington, became one of the healthiest cities in America due to his healing rooms!

THE ROD OF AUTHORITY

Beginning with the fourth chapter of Exodus, we read:

> *Moses answered and said, "But suppose they will not believe me or listen to my voice; suppose they say, 'The Lord has not appeared to you.'" So the Lord said to him, "What is that in your hand?" He said, "A rod." And He said, "Cast it on the ground." So he cast it on the ground, and it became a serpent; and Moses fled from it. Then the Lord said to Moses, "Reach out your hand and take it by the tail" (and he reached out his hand and caught it, and it became a rod in his hand) (Exodus 4:1-4).*

The rod represents divine power and authority that was to be released through Moses on behalf of the children of Israel.

I believe God is releasing power and authority in this hour; I see a new breed of ministers who are being mantled with governmental authority and power!

God had raised up Moses, for a purpose. The purpose of governmental mantling is to bring freedom to the masses and reveal the plan of God on the earth.

ENDNOTES

1. Charles Spurgeon, *An All-Round Ministry* (Edinburgh, Scotland: Banner of Truth, 1960).
2. John G. Lake, *John G. Lake on Healing.*

ACTIVATION PRAYER

Father, I thank You for using me to establish Your Kingdom on the earth. Use me to demonstrate Your love and power to all those I encounter. I declare that Your glory will be shown through miracles, signs, and wonders in my city and region. Thank You for setting me before kings and princes, and for giving me favor with men and women in high positions, that I may display Your goodness, power, and love!

ABOUT THE AUTHORS

Jesse and Amy Shamp are a powerful itinerant ministry based in Nashville, Tennessee. Their mission is to edify and equip the body of Christ for the work of the ministry. Signs, wonders, and miracles follow their ministry, and they often receive powerful prophetic dreams from God for the Church. They are committed to crusade evangelism and are passionate about bringing in a harvest in the nations. Jesse received his doctorate degree and Amy received her bachelor's degree from the International Miracle Institute in Pensacola, Florida.